UNDAUNTED

UNDAUNTED

DARING TO DO WHAT GOD
CALLS YOU TO DO

CHRISTINE CAINE

ZONDERVAN

Undaunted
Copyright © 2012, 2019 by Christine Caine and Equip and Empower Ministries

Requests for information should be addressed to:
Zondervan, *3900 Sparks Dr. SE, Grand Rapids, Michigan 49546*

ISBN 978-0-310-35588-5 (softcover)

ISBN 978-0-310-35590-8 (audio)

ISBN 978-0-310-35589-2 (ebook)

Library of Congress Cataloging-in-Publication Data

Caine, Christine.
     Undaunted : daring to do what God calls you to do / Christine Caine.
        p. cm.
     Includes bibliographical references.
     ISBN 978-0-310-33387-6 (Softcover)
     1. Self-actualization (Psychology)--Religious aspects--Christianity. 2. Power
(Christian theology) 3. Human trafficking--Prevention. 4. Church work with
prostitutes. 5. Prostitutes--Religious life. I. Title.
BV4598.2.C355 2012
248.4--dc23   2012016762

Published in association with the literary agency of David O. Middlebrook, 4501 Merlot Avenue, Grapevine, Texas, 76051.

Cover design: Curt Diepenhorst
Cover photo: Nate Griffin
Interior design: Kait Lamphere

Printed in the United States of America

19 20 21 22 23 24 25 26 27 28 /LSC/ 15 14 13 12 11 10 9 8 7 6 5 4 3 2 1

To my husband, Nick, and precious daughters,
Catherine and Sophia.

You are God's greatest gifts to me.

With *undaunted* faith Abraham looked at the facts—his own impotence (he was practically a hundred years old at the time) and his wife Sarah's apparent barrenness. Yet he refused to allow any distrust of a definite pronouncement of God to make him waver. He drew strength from his faith, and while giving the glory to God, remained absolutely convinced that God was able to implement his own promise. This was the "faith" which "was accounted to him for righteousness."

—ROMANS 4:19–22 (PHILLIPS)

CONTENTS

Part 3:
GOD KNOWS MY FEAR

Part 4:
GOD KNOWS MY DESTINY

FOREWORD

I've wondered what it would be like to visit with the apostle Paul—the globe-trotting, gospel-proclaiming, chain-breaking trumpeter of grace.

I've imagined a good chat with Mary, the mother of Jesus—the simple village girl who, upon learning that she would be virgin *and* pregnant, told God, "Whatever you say, I'll do."

I've envisioned a conversation with Esther, the liberator from nowhere. Out of the shadows she stepped, and because she did, a nation was spared.

Paul. Mary. Esther. Turns out, I've met all three in the person of Christine Caine.

She has the spunk of a Paul. She's scarcely on the stage, or at the dinner table, before you hear her passions: Jesus, her family, and the forgotten girls of the slave trade. You know where she stands. And you know whom she loves. It's contagious, this heart of hers. Wonderfully infectious.

She has the obedience of a Mary. Who would have pegged a Greek-born, Australia-raised, blonde pistol as a world-changer?

Yet just like the mother of Jesus, she brings Christ to the nations. Everywhere Christine goes, from South Africa to Eastern

Europe, she radiates hope. Especially to the girls to whom she is an Esther—the millions of teenage girls who find themselves in the throes of Satan's cruelest concoction, the sex trade. These young women should be becoming exactly that, young women. They should be listening to music, reading books, and flirting with guys. Instead they are locked into brothels, beaten, raped, and treated like livestock.

Their only hope? Jesus Christ. And Jesus has chosen to work through people like Christine. Christ appears, not just in her name but in her face, resolve, grit, and joy. She makes the rest of us want to love the Jesus she loves in the manner she loves him.

I pray you will read this book. If and when you do, you'll discover what I have: God has given our generation a Paul, Mary, and Esther. And her name is Christine Caine.

God has given our generation the opportunity to make a difference in the vilest atrocity of the century.

After reading this book, I resolve to do more.

I hope you will too.

—*Max Lucado*

PREFACE

In 2018, Nick and I, and our team, celebrated the ten-year anniversary of A21, our global anti–human trafficking organization. When I first wrote this book, we had only just started. We knew God had called us to make a difference, so with one office and a handful of team members, we began. We had no real idea what we were doing or how to move forward most days, but we did have passion, commitment, a willingness to learn, and much-needed undaunted faith. We approached each day doing the only thing we knew to do—get up, pray with a holy desperation, put one foot in front of the other, and trust God to make a way and direct our paths. We researched, we asked questions, and we stumbled along, often taking two steps forward only to take three steps back. When we encountered one seemingly impossible obstacle after another, we felt like giving up, and yet, by God's grace and strength, we kept going—one day at a time, one step at a time, to rescue one life at a time. It really has always been about the one. We have always wanted to do our part to help abolish slavery everywhere, forever.

Since then, so much has changed, and we have grown and expanded our reach around the globe. When I originally wrote this book, I thought I understood undaunted faith and I felt I had a lot to say, but since then, I have learned so much more. I have been stretched, challenged, and changed in ways I never thought possible, and my faith has grown. As a result, I felt compelled to revise this book and expand it.

I have loved reliving so many details, rewriting the stories to include more, and even adding new ones that will inspire you to step into your God-given purpose. We are living in such challenging days, when there is so much chaos, division, pain, confusion, and suffering in our world, that if we are to be the witnesses God has called us to be in our generation, then we will need to step into the future undaunted.

Inside these pages is a message for every single one of us. So turn the page and start reading. I believe you will be inspired to live undaunted.

—Love,
Chris

Chapter 1

HE HAS CALLED US

"Why didn't you come sooner? If what you are telling me is true, if what you say about your God is true, then where were you?" Sonia demanded. Her voice, which had been rich with a beautiful Russian accent minutes before, had grown thick with emotion, almost taut from a simmering rage, and it pierced my heart: "Where have you been?"

Sitting in a circle of young women who recently had been rescued from sex trafficking, who had been used and abused in vile ways, forced to grow much older than their years, I had hoped to encourage them and show them genuine love. But my words, which seemed to penetrate their hearts only moments ago and give them a glimpse of God's unconditional love and mercy, were being thrown right back at me in one explosive blow after another. Sonia had just been the bravest in the room, brave enough to confront me, to voice what they all were thinking.

"Why didn't you come sooner?" she insisted. It was a raw and honest question that deserved a substantive answer.

Staring back at her, feeling the pressure of the moment, I leaned into the heart of God for the answer. I searched for how to respond to her, for how to answer all of them. While I waited, while they waited, no one moved. No one uttered a word. No one took their eyes off me. And I felt that her heartbreaking cry for an answer would reverberate in my head forever.

Why didn't you come sooner?

As I looked into her eyes, I could see all the anguish they exposed, and my desperation to answer her softened into feelings of compassion I had never known. I shuddered at all she had shared, a nineteen-year-old trapped in a room for one year, forced to service at least twenty-five men every day. Wrecked by her pain, I could see so many more of the young women I'd met, women just like Sonia. All their stories of being poor, starving, unable to feed or protect their families flooded my thoughts. They were easy prey for the traffickers who had exploited their vulnerabilities. I remembered so many of them, depressed, suicidal, desperate to end their suffering. I remembered the children I'd met, languishing and dying from malnutrition, many sold into slavery sometimes as early as their toddler years. Their faces blurred together—hundreds, thousands, millions. Too many to count. Too many to see clearly. They melded into an ocean of floating faces, bobbing in and out of focus. Hazy. Distorted. In a depth of suffering, loneliness, need, despondency, and hopelessness I'd never known. And then they were sinking, and I could hear their cries until they were so faint that they were no more.

Why didn't I come sooner? How can I possibly help Sonia forgive, be healed, and be restored to a life that God wants to give her? Jesus, help me. How should I answer her?

SHATTERED DREAMS

When I arrived in Greece twenty-four hours before, it wasn't the Greece that I remembered from my honeymoon fourteen years earlier. There were no stunning, whitewashed buildings, no lapis-blue tile rooftops. There was no festive music. No outdoor market with vendors selling freshly pressed olive oil, mouthwatering feta cheese, or fresh cantaloupe.

Instead I found the Greece of March 2010 still reeling from the 2008 financial crisis that had struck the world. Affected by the plummeting of the US market, all of Europe had entered a recession, and Greece had suffered the most.[1] Now the streets were empty, black, and wet. Even the crystal-blue Aegean Sea seemed to reflect the dismal state of affairs. Driving past the port, staring at the cold sea, watching it thrash about, I could feel how the fear of economic collapse had changed everything, and I couldn't help but wonder, *Is this how they see it? Their lives? Their futures?*

"They" were fourteen young women, mostly Eastern European, who had been rescued by A21. Young women who were mere schoolgirls when they were lured from their homes in the Ukraine, Bulgaria, Georgia, Albania, Romania, Russia, Uzbekistan, and even an African nation. Sixteen-, seventeen-, eighteen-year-olds. Girls who should have been giggling about music and basketball games, worrying about what to wear to school, not how to survive being held captive as slaves.

In a home in a part of Greece I'd never known, I had come to visit them, encourage them, and remind them that they were safe. But when I met with them, it seemed that all I had done was stir up the horrors of their pain. One by one, they braved telling me of unspeakable shame and agony, of unfathomable evil done to them.

Nadia was the first to tell me her story. She recounted how she had been raised in a village in Georgia during a time of war and deprivation. Her family possessed an abundance of love but not food. Poverty consumed them. For years, Nadia lived on dreams— dreams of escaping hunger, dreams of a world far away from the ravaged village, dreams of becoming a nurse. If she were a nurse, she explained, like the ones she saw dressing the wounds of soldiers in her village, she could get away. She could travel and see a beautiful world, a world in which she would have a helpful role to play.

But girls in poor Georgian villages did not go to school beyond second grade. They needed to learn only how to cook and clean, not read and write. In their culture, no man would want to marry a woman more educated than he. She was expected to marry, keep house, bear children, and depend on her husband for everything.

Nadia, an obedient daughter who desperately wanted to please her parents, tried to push aside her secret dreams. Yet embers still burned in her heart.

So just three weeks before her seventeenth birthday, when a man approached her group of friends at their bus stop and told them of opportunities to work in Greece, those embers couldn't help but glow brighter. The man told them that Greece was beautiful and that the people prospered there. He said there were many good-paying jobs for waitresses, hairdressers, and shop assistants. He said there were jobs just waiting for nurses. He somehow knew exactly what to say.

The man gave her a brochure and invited her to a meeting the following Friday evening, where he would provide all of the details.

For the next week, Nadia was blinded by the light of opportunity. Her dreams suddenly seemed so possible, so attainable. So on Friday, she arrived early at the village community hall and found a seat in the front row. Several dozen other girls trickled in after her, filling the room with their excited chatter. Some men, including the one who had given Nadia a brochure, introduced themselves as agents and gave a compelling presentation of the opportunities in Greece. They promised a bright future. They passed out paperwork for obtaining passports and work visas and patiently helped the girls fill out the forms.

Nadia left the community hall overflowing with hope. She ran home to tell her parents about her amazing chance to start a new life. Not only could she get an education and training as a nurse and live her dream of helping others, she could also soon send money home to her entire family.

Her parents were concerned, though. Greece was so far away. They didn't know these men or whether they could be trusted. But her compelling passion ignited the embers of hope in their hearts. Perhaps their daughter would be able to get ahead as they never had.

Perhaps she could find a profession and earn a good income. She could be their key to new lives too.

After much discussion, they reluctantly agreed to let her go, even draining all their accounts, selling what they could, and borrowing what was necessary to scrape together the fee Nadia needed to pay the hiring agents for her passage to Greece. Her dreams of happiness, success, and newfound prosperity became their dreams too.

A week later, when Nadia waved goodbye to her parents, she had no idea she might never see them again.

Landing at the airport in Greece, Nadia was met by a woman from the hiring agency who spoke no Russian. Nadia spoke no Greek. But despite the language challenges and ensuing confusion, Nadia apprehensively went with the woman to an apartment building, where she was shown a room that was supposed to be hers. Then the woman left Nadia to unpack and settle in.

But within minutes, her world unraveled and a nightmare unfolded. Several men rushed in and locked the door behind them. They beat and raped Nadia repeatedly. She tried to fight back. She screamed for help until her vocal cords could no longer make a sound. And for every protest she voiced, for every scream she uttered, she received even more abuse, more torture.

Confused, scared, ashamed, in pain, and broken, Nadia retreated internally into a dark, deep place that would take her years to escape.

For the next two weeks, the beatings and rape continued, until there was nothing left of the girl and her dreams, until the girl she once was surrendered to a cruel force she couldn't fight.

That's when the agents told Nadia about her new job—the one they'd schemed for her all along. It wasn't in a hospital. It wasn't in a restaurant. It wasn't in a store. It was in a brothel. Her new life was to be a sex slave. "If you do not do as we tell you, we will kill your family," they said.

For Nadia, it was enough. By then she was convinced that these people were so evil that they would make good on their threat.

They had taken her papers, including her passport. She didn't speak Greek. She had no idea where she was. Even if she somehow found a way to escape, where would she go? She knew she wouldn't make it far, let alone all the way back to Georgia. She was utterly alone, though the men she had believed were hiring agents surrounded her twenty-four hours a day, seven days a week. When they weren't in her room, they stood guard outside her door and sent in a constant flow of customers with whom she was forced to perform unmentionable acts—up to forty times a day.

No longer sure there was a God in heaven—because why would he have allowed this to happen?—Nadia pleaded with God anyway. *Let me die,* she prayed over and over. *Let me die. Oblivion would be better than this.* The trauma and the horror continued to pull her deeper and deeper and deeper into utter despair. And as hopelessness settled in, all the embers of her dreams were snuffed out. There was no hope of ever returning to a life with her family, to things familiar and free.

But one day, when a guard left her room, he forgot to lock the window. Though her room was on the third floor of the apartment building, Nadia scrambled onto the balcony. *Maybe, if I am lucky, the impact will kill me. Oh, God,* she prayed, *let the nightmare end.*

She jumped.

A woman who was passing by saw Nadia throw herself from the third-story balcony and crash onto the pavement. Horrified, she ran to Nadia, who, miraculously, was uninjured.

As the woman fretted over Nadia, asking her if she was all right, Nadia was amazed that she understood. Had she died? Was she in heaven? No. It was a miracle. The woman was real. And she spoke Russian! She wanted to help Nadia. Quickly Nadia told her the nightmare that she'd been living.

The woman pulled Nadia up from the pavement and rushed her to the police station. There the police took her statement, and then they moved her to a secure location to protect her. Soon she was put in contact with our A21 team.

WHEN THE BUBBLE BROKE

One by one that March afternoon, the girls around me shared their stories, all versions of Nadia's nightmare. Most had been raised in impoverished, formerly communist Eastern European nations. Each had come to Greece expecting legitimate employment. All had brought with them hope to do something more with their lives than their parents had ever thought possible. But all of their tender, youthful dreams had been stolen and shattered.

What shook me most was the realization that, for each of these young women whom I spoke to that day, there were millions of others still trapped in slavery, millions of women whose unspeakable pain remained shrouded in secrecy. Millions of women suffering in silence. Somewhere.

When Maria told her story, she described how she and more than fifty other young women had come to Greece in a shipping container.

"Wait," I interrupted. "Do you mean you were contained in a ship?" I thought that I'd misunderstood or that something had been lost in translation.

Maria repeated: she and more than fifty other young women were brought to Greece in a shipping container.

A container loaded onto a ship? Like the one that a moving company was going to use to ship my household goods to our new home? "A box?" I pressed. "A container used to carry personal and commercial goods, not people?"

That's right, Maria assured me—a box, a container put onto a ship. When she and the other girls arrived at the port the day of their departure, just like Nadia and her friends, they thought they were traveling to good-paying jobs in a land of opportunity. Instead they were greeted by hiring agents who said that there had been complications with their paperwork and that they had only one choice: travel by container or lose their deposits and any opportunity to work abroad. Make the voyage in a shipping container or turn around and go home.

"Our families had given everything they owned to pay for our passage," Maria said.

So one by one, bewildered and frightened, the girls entered the container. When the last girl was inside, the door was slammed shut and they heard a lock clang against the metal. They sat fearfully frozen in the darkness.

"Then the bubble broke! The bubble broke!" Maria exclaimed.

"What bubble?"

The air filter, she explained, that allowed oxygen to circulate in the container. It stopped working, and the inside of the cramped box suddenly became a suffocating coffin.

I gasped, imagining the oxygen being rapidly depleted, the heat building, the women gulping for air in complete darkness.

The journey in the sealed container was gruesome. Half the girls died early on from lack of oxygen. The other half, the stronger ones, teetered on the edge of death. They had nowhere to sit but in their own vomit and feces, since they were forced to relieve themselves on the container's floor.

When the men at port opened the container, Maria said, they recoiled, appalled by the smell of death, decay, and excrement.

One of the dead was Anna, Maria's best friend. Anna had died an excruciating death, suffocating as if buried alive. Anna was real, Maria insisted to me that day. Anna had existed. And Anna must be remembered.

The hiring agents preferred to forget. More interested in quickly getting what they referred to as their shipped goods from the dockyard, they hustled the remaining girls to small apartments nearby, where, like Nadia, the girls were repeatedly raped and beaten.

Before sunrise one morning, Maria said, after she had lost all sense of time, the girls were loaded into small rubber boats and taken across the Mediterranean Sea to a Greek island. This was the first time they realized that their voyage had not even taken them to Greece. They had been brutalized in Turkey. None of the agents had kept their promises.

In the boat, Maria felt a surge of hope. The Greek Coast Guard was doing a routine check that morning—unusual for that hour, Maria later learned. She hoped that, unlike the crew on the docks, the Coast Guard could not be bribed to turn a blind eye. Maria's captors showed signs of panic. Though Maria was freezing, deprived of sleep and food, broken, and in shock, her hope grew. Rescue! Justice! Once caught, the traffickers would face a lengthy imprisonment.

And for that reason, these men would do anything to avoid being caught.

They began throwing the girls overboard.

Only a few of the thirty or so girls—those who had been strong enough to survive the deadly voyage in the shipping container—escaped drowning that day.

Those few were spared because they were able to be hidden among their captors when the Coast Guard came aboard. When the boat finally arrived in Athens, the girls were taken to a brothel, where the nightmare of the Turkish apartment continued. Daily, Maria and the others were forced to participate in unspeakable encounters with dozens of men. Maria sank deeper into despair, wishing that she too had suffocated in the container or drowned in the Mediterranean Sea.

The horror continued for weeks. Or maybe it was months. Maria wasn't sure anymore. But one day, anti-trafficking authorities, responding to a tip, raided the brothel. Maria and other girls were herded into the back of what appeared to be a police van. Were they being rescued? If hiring agents could be evil, couldn't police be as well? Uncertain and broken, Maria didn't get her hopes up when she and a dozen other girls were raced to another apartment building. Police rushed them inside, where they waited in fear and resignation. But instead of beatings and rape, they were given rest, food, water, and a sense of peace.

Though no longer in captivity, Maria remained silent in a prison she couldn't escape, constantly tormented by nightmares. The daily horror may have ceased, but the pain screamed nonstop.

Maria was indeed safe, but not yet free.

MY SCHINDLER'S LIST MOMENT

Stunned, I sat quietly for a moment after Maria finished her story. Around me, the young women remained quiet too, almost reverent. Yet inside me, a storm raged and questions hammered at my broken heart. *How could this possibly happen in our world today? No matter how much money is involved, how could anyone be so depraved as to sell human beings again and again and again?*

And that's when Sonia called me out. That's when she interrupted my thoughts with her demand.

"Why are you here? Why did you come?"

And when I took a breath to grapple for an answer, she pressed in further, glaring at me with well-deserved distrust. "Why didn't you come sooner? If what you are telling me is true, then where were you? Where have you been?"

That's when the pounding in both my heart and my head grew louder than anything else in the room.

Why didn't you come sooner?

Truthfully, I hadn't known. I hadn't known of the horrific nightmare they were living or where they were or what evil was befalling them. How could I have come before I knew? How could I intervene in something that I didn't know existed? I simply didn't know until I did know. And then I responded. That's when Nick and I founded A21 in 2008. Yes, the same year as the worst global economic crisis since the Stock Market Crash of 1929.[2] And God didn't just tell us to rescue victims of human trafficking, he gave us a vision for a complete work—from rescue all the way to restoration, to give victims not only healthcare and emotional support but housing and education, hope for a complete future.

But Sonia didn't care about any of that. Not today. And I wouldn't offer any excuses. How could I? How dare I? Sitting there, surrounded by them, I couldn't help but feel overwhelmed by their pain, by their suffering at the hands of cruel men. I couldn't help but see the scars imprinted on their souls.

Looking at her, at all of them, it felt so surreal, yet all too real, to be sitting there, absorbing all they had shared. Inside I leaned into God even further. *Tell me what to say. Tell me how to bring your healing and restoration.*

In seconds, a scene from *Schindler's List* flashed into my mind. At the end of that movie, Oskar Schindler, a gentile businessman in Nazi Germany who saved the lives of more than a thousand Jews by breaking the law to keep them working in his factories, is being thanked for what he has done by a crowd of those he has rescued, just before he flees for his own life. The grateful Jews present him with a gold ring on the inside of which is inscribed a saying from the Talmud: "Whoever saves one life saves the world entire."

But distressed, Schindler says, "I could have got more out. I could have got more. I don't know . . . if I had just . . . I threw away so much money. You have no idea . . . I didn't do enough."

He looks at his car. "Why did I keep the car? Ten people right there."

He pulls a pin from his lapel. "This pin. This is gold. Two more people . . . and I didn't. I didn't."

And then he collapses into tears, overcome by the realization not of all that he *did* but that the pin in his lapel was apparently worth more to him than the lives of two people.

This moment, sitting at that table in Thessaloniki with those women so recently saved from slavery and yet still so devastated by it, was my *Schindler's List* moment. It was my moment of wondering what, in my life, had been my golden pin, the thing so precious to me that it never occurred to me to use it to ransom someone else's life.

Whoever saves one life saves the world entire.

Though I felt like Maria in that container, the weight of such a heartfelt cry pressing in on me like suffocating, airless darkness, though I felt like I could barely breathe, I would not offer excuses. I would stand up and fight for them, fight with them, and help them be restored. I would answer them undaunted. Full of faith. Full of hope. Even in the face of their having none.

"I don't know," I stammered at last. "I don't know why I didn't come sooner." Such weak, small, light words for such a weighty question. "I am sorry. I am so sorry. Please forgive me."

The silence became even more pronounced. Time seemed to stop. And nothing else mattered to me at that moment but these girls and their despair and the healing God could bring to them. Though the silence seemed to last for an eternity, I felt so clearly present, so tuned in to the now.

"I want you to know," I said with conviction, "that I have now heard your cries. I have seen you. I see you now."

I turned to Maria. "I *see* you, Maria. And when I see you, I see Anna."

I turned to Sonia. "I see you, Sonia."

I looked intently at each girl seated at the table. "I see each of you. I hear you. I know you by name. I have come for each of you."

I wanted to see these girls as Jesus saw them—not as a sea of needs but as individuals whom he had called by name and chosen one by one and loved. I heard his words before I spoke my own. *Tell them I have their names written in my book. That I came to give the good news to the poor. To heal the brokenhearted. To set the captives free. Tell them these promises are for here. Now. As well as for eternity.*[3]

"You will no longer be hidden," I told Sonia. "From now on, wherever I go, I will tell people you exist." Looking around the circle once more, I focused on each girl, one at a time. "I will ask them the very same question that you've asked me. I will not sit back waiting, hoping, wishing for someone else to do something. I promise you: I will *be* the someone. Now that I have found you, I will find other girls like you. I will do everything I can to stop this."

HE HAS CALLED YOU

Long after I left the girls, Sonia's question consumed me. *Why didn't you come sooner?*

I offered them no excuses that day, but I did know that there were reasons. Humanity needed to do more to stop such evil. God called me and I answered and I got there as fast as I knew how. And I knew even more were called to help, because we're all called to do something. We're all called to fulfill a purpose, to reach a destiny, to be all that God created us to be and to do all that God created us to do. Our calling is that God-given passion that can never be quenched, that assignment we were born to fulfill.

When Paul wrote to the church in Rome, he began his letter by saying that he was "a servant of Christ Jesus, called to be an apostle." The word *called* in this verse carries a sense of purpose, intent, and direction. When Paul heard God's divine call on the road to Damascus, he was flooded with a powerful sense of destiny.[4]

Part of my calling is to share the gospel and to see people come to Christ. I'm called to teach the Word of God so people can be transformed by the power of God. I'm called to lead and teach others to lead so they can learn how to be full of the power of God, so they can fulfill what God has called them to do. I'm called to be a wife and a mother. A friend. And I'm called to help abolish slavery everywhere, forever.

These callings are my assignments, my vocations. The word *vocation* is from the Latin *vocatio*, which means "calling." At its core, work is calling, designed by God to fulfill a purpose that is outside of oneself, a purpose that brings glory to God and blesses others. We were all created for work. Even before God gave Adam a spouse, he assigned him a vocation, a calling. He was to tend the garden and name the animals.[5]

God called me to reach the Sonias, Nadias, Annas, and Marias of this world. And I answered that call, though I felt unqualified.

But don't we all feel that way when God calls us to do something? Whether it's to start a business, launch an outreach, or walk across the street to meet a new neighbor and spark a friendship, when God's Spirit gently nudges us—or not so gently nudges us— to make a bold step, take a risk, serve others, save a life, or commit, why is it that we so often hold back? At least a little?

Because we don't feel empowered.

We don't feel qualified.

We think we lack the courage, the strength, the wisdom, the money, the influence, the experience, the education, the organization, the backing. We feel like Moses when, from out of the burning bush, God called him to speak for him before Pharaoh—the highest leader in the land. And Moses answered, "Pardon your servant, Lord. I have never been eloquent. . . . I am slow of speech and tongue. . . . Please send someone else."[6]

We can sound just like that when God calls us. *Not me, God. I'm afraid. Weak. Poor. Incapable. Unqualified. Daunted.*

There were years of my life when that's exactly how I would have responded, but by the time I met Sonia, Nadia, and Maria, I had surrendered my life to Jesus and grown to live *un*daunted.

Yet even when I was younger and consumed by fear, I didn't want to be daunted, to be afraid, intimidated, or discouraged by difficulty, danger, or disappointment. I didn't want to be unable to respond to God's call. And I doubt that's your desire either. I think that you, like me, want to be able to say instead, "Here am I, Lord—send me." We don't want to sound like Moses, stammering in search of excuses.

And the truth is, we don't need to, because just as God gave Moses exactly what he needed to accomplish great things, he wants to equip us just as profoundly. If he calls us to slay giants, then he will be sure to make us into giant slayers. God doesn't call the qualified. He qualifies the called.

He leads us in how to live undaunted so we can fulfill our calling. To live undaunted is to show courage and resolution. It's to live unafraid, undismayed, unflinching, unshrinking, unabashed. It's to be bold, brave, gritty, audacious, daring, and confident—even when we face opportunities not to be.

Trust me, life won't disappoint when it comes to challenging us, to intimidating us. There is no shortage of ways the enemy will try to daunt us, to render us incapable of following the bold and valiant plan God has for us. But God has called us to live undaunted. To live boldly and courageously in the face of difficulty and to amaze the world by beating the odds, all for his glory.

And as I left Thessaloniki after meeting those girls, I thought of my own story. If anyone ever had a reason to feel unqualified, to feel daunted, it was me. The reasons for that went back to things that happened before I was even born, back to things I had no control over that created obstacles that should have landed me in a much different place. I want to share my story with you, because I believe it will inspire you to learn as I did to live undaunted.

Note: While the stories told in this chapter are based on fact, details and the names of the women have been altered to protect their identities and to ensure their continued safety.

PART 1

GOD KNOWS MY NAME

Chapter 2

I'M NOT WHO I THOUGHT I WAS

I had just closed my mouth around that first, long-awaited forkful of beef vindaloo—extra spicy—when my cell phone rang. Looking down at my phone, blocking out the midday chaos of the office dining area, I saw that it was Kathy, my sister-in-law. I savored the steaming vindaloo and considered letting her leave a message on voicemail. No. She rarely called in the middle of the day.

You'll just have to wait, I told my impatient stomach. I set down my fork and answered my phone.

The moment that I heard Kathy's voice, I knew something was wrong. "Christine, George needs you. Can you talk to him? He's very upset. He just received a letter from the Social Services Department that claims he's not your biological sibling. He was adopted at birth by your parents."

What! I couldn't believe what I was hearing. "Let me talk with him," I said.

George came on the line, quite distraught. He recounted what Kathy had said, and then he read the letter to me. "What do you make of this?" he desperately asked.

"It's got to be a mistake," I immediately decided. "Social Services obviously sent this to the wrong person. Call the supervisors at Social Services immediately and tell them about this. Tell them it has to be a mistake. Then call me back to let me know how it went."

I hung up and pushed away my plate of food. The beef vindaloo that had seemed so delicious a few minutes before now didn't interest me at all.

How could someone have been so careless? Didn't they realize that a mistake like this could turn someone's world upside down? Why hadn't they taken more care in addressing the envelope or in noticing which envelope they stuffed the letter into?

Moments later my phone rang again, interrupting the storm brewing inside me. "George!"

He was breathless, his voice trembling. "Christine, it's true. They have an entire file on me. They told me that my birth mother has been trying to contact me, and they gave me the name of my biological mother and father. They told me where I was born. I have an appointment to go in and see the Social Services people tomorrow. They said they will tell me everything."

"It *can't* be true, George!" My racing heart beat over the sound of his mounting confusion. "This is just a big mistake, a mess. We'll get it straightened out." Though I tried to sound confident, I felt my own confusion and concern rising with his.

An entire file . . .

"I have to talk to Mum about this," George said. "I can't wait. I'm going over there now."

I told him I would meet him there.

Snatching up my purse, I raced toward the parking lot, my mind spinning faster than I was running. *It's impossible—of course George is my brother. We grew up together. It's a ridiculous mistake. But . . . what if it is true? After all, there's an entire file—no! It can't be true. What's George going to say to Mum?*

I was so shaken that for a full five minutes I couldn't remember where I'd left my vehicle. I scanned the parking lot over and over, eventually finding it right where I had parked it. I jumped in and drove to Mum's house in record time. For the second time that afternoon, I found myself bracing for an unexpected encounter I couldn't control.

THE DAY EVERYTHING CHANGED

As I walked up the path to the front door, I thought about all the years of memories our family had created together in this home. The endless afternoon soccer games with friends in our front yard. The gathering place for all the kids in the neighborhood. The birthday cakes and homework dug into at the kitchen table. The Christmases around the tree. *How could all of that not have been just what it seemed to us then—a normal family living life together? And yet what if this letter George received is true? Is everything about to change?*

Oh, God, I prayed, *give me wisdom, guidance, grace, and patience.* As I stepped through the doorway, I froze at what I saw. Kathy was standing just behind George as he was handing Mum the letter from Social Services.

I could see Mum's hands begin to shake as she scanned it.

Watching her, I realized there was genuine fear, not confusion, in her eyes. And that's when I knew. *It's true*, I thought. *It's true. My brother is adopted.* Time seemed to stop. I felt as though I couldn't breathe, as though I were pinned in place and able only to helplessly watch as tears streamed down Mum's face.

As I moved my gaze to George, my chest ached at seeing how utterly heartbroken he was. Mum finally choked out words. "I am so sorry you found out like this, George. We never meant to hurt you. We love you. I couldn't have loved you more if I had given birth to you myself. We loved you before we even laid eyes on you, and once we did, at the hospital, we never considered you anyone else's but ours. A closed adoption was the only option we were given, at your birth mother's insistence, and we were advised to never tell you that you were anything else but our very own. I never imagined that your birth mother would try to contact you or be allowed to. She signed a form giving you to us totally. I don't understand! The adoption laws must have changed."

Mum looked down at the letter, slowly shaking her head in disbelief. She sobbed, repeating, "I couldn't have loved you more. I couldn't have loved you more."

Then, "We didn't want you to even think you were unwanted or rejected. We never dreamed you could find out, especially after all of these years. One of the last things I promised your father before he died was that I would never tell you."

I felt paralyzed. Her words were beautiful, breathtaking, filled with devotion. But the scene playing before me seemed so surreal, more like a movie than my own life. Than George's life. *How could this secret have been kept from my brother for thirty-five years? How could Mum and Dad never have told us that George was adopted? Why have I never had the slightest suspicion that George and I are not biological siblings?*

And yet.

This explained the mystery of why George is six foot four and I am five foot three. And why I have perfectly straight light hair, while he has curly dark hair. I almost laughed at how absurd it now seemed. *How could I have overlooked such glaring dissimilarities all these years?* But then, just as quickly, a sudden thought sobered me. *What other family secrets do I not know?*

The question overwhelmed me. The tension, fears, and tears were rising among us all, so I decided to do what any good Greek girl would do in the eye of a storm.

I headed straight to the kitchen to prepare something for everyone to eat.

Raised according to the philosophy that food is the answer to most things, I functioned on autopilot to make extra-strong Greek coffee and rummage in the pantry for some baklava. Our heritage had taught me that when in doubt about what to do or say, turn to cooking and eating, and a solution will present itself. So I set everything on the table, hoping the combination of caffeine and sugar would recalibrate us. Then I took a deep breath and called to George, Kathy, and Mum.

We gathered around the same table where our family had shared meals and ordinary moments and milestones for more than twenty years. The daily events that create bonds of love that seemingly can never be separated. But now, in one afternoon, the atmosphere around our table had changed. Our trust had been breached. There was a schism where before there had been none. We sat on the edge of it, so shaken that we didn't know where or how things were going to settle or whether more things would crumble and fall. Uncertainty clung in the air and in the pit of my stomach. With one letter, with a single seismic conversation, everything that I thought I knew about our family had been turned upside down and inside out.

THE WHOLE TRUTH

For a few awkward moments, we all sipped our coffee. Then Mum cried as she began telling us the story she never had, of how after several years of trying unsuccessfully to conceive, she and Dad had been given an opportunity to adopt. They had decided to take it, while continuing to try to have children naturally. It had been a time of great anticipation, she said, repeating, "We loved you before you were born. We loved you before we laid eyes on you."

I realized that, amazingly, neighbors and extended family members must have known, yet not one of them said anything about it to us kids. *How can you keep such a thing secret? You can't exactly hide one day not being pregnant and the next coming home with a baby! How was it possible that so many people knew about this for decades yet over the years never let a hint slip?*

And yet.

And yet there *had* been hints, though they had been unclear to me at the time. I remembered an incident around this same kitchen table when I was eleven years old. Mum had been peeling onions, preparing our dinner, as George and I and our younger brother, Andrew, played the board game Trouble. Somehow our conversation turned to adoption. I'm not sure how that happened, but I remember telling Mum that even if I were adopted, I wouldn't care, because I loved her and Dad so.

"I can't even imagine anyone else being my parents," I remembered saying.

My brothers each had echoed my comments. *I can't even imagine anyone else being my parents.*

I drew in a long breath. And for all these years, I had thought it was the onions that made Mum cry that day. Dad had called on the phone a few minutes later as we three kids continued our board game, and Mum told him that we had been talking about adoption. She left the room as she talked, and her voice dropped to a whisper. *What is it that I'm not supposed to know?* I wondered at the time. *What is it that they don't want me to hear?*

I strained, unsuccessfully, to eavesdrop but heard nothing. Impatient, my brothers whined that it was my turn to play, and I turned back to our game as Mum returned to the kitchen. She busied herself with the pans as she prepared dinner. And that was that. From that moment until this, the word *adoption* was never again mentioned in our home.

Now, as George sat with his head in his hands, struggling to make sense of this new reality, I looked at Mum and said, "That day . . ." I wanted to know now what was kept from me back then. "Remember that day?" I said as I searched her face.

Mum nodded. She knew. "I remember every detail." She told us how she'd come undone by the very mention of the word she and Dad had worked so hard to keep us from hearing, from understanding, from suspecting. When Dad called, she was ready to collapse from the stress of it all.

"Shouldn't we tell them?" she'd pressed.

She and Dad had reasoned together. The truth might hurt us.

Maybe it was best to keep things as they were, they agreed, and never speak of it again.

Now here it was, that secret truth, being spilled out at the same kitchen table. But with the confession now over, Mum's face had relaxed. Her tension eased. She seemed relieved, freed by the truth that was now in the open.

And yet for the other three of us, the tension remained. We were still reeling from the effects of such a revelation. Kathy was motionless. George sat speechless. I was still trying to determine whether he was going to be okay. Looking at him, I thought, *He's in shock.*

Then the silence, the stillness, took on an energy of its own. To break the strain, I reached for another piece of baklava.

"Christine?" Mum asked. "Since we're telling the truth, would you like to know the whole truth?"

I dropped the baklava.

My heart skipped a beat, possibly five. The way she had asked that question could mean only one thing. I searched her eyes, hoping for some sign that I was wrong. *Please let it not be true.* Finally, I choked out, "I was adopted too."

How much more bizarre could this day become?

What do you do when you have been living all your life, more than three decades, with facts that you thought were true, only to discover that so many of them weren't facts at all?

What else in my life was a lie? What other secrets were there about our family, about the life I thought I knew so well? Could I trust anyone or anything else? I felt like I was living in my own version of the movie *The Truman Show.*

Remember that film? How Truman discovered that his home, workplace, and world were not real at all but rather constructed as part of a television studio that contained hidden cameras everywhere? Truman began to suspect, and then proved, that his friends and associates, from best friend to mailman to man on the street, were merely actors, each hired to play a fictional role in his pretend, though unscripted, life. Everyone around him knew that his life was merely *The Truman Show,* the most popular television series in the world. Everyone knew, that is, except Truman. I thought about how he discovered the lie, the hidden cameras, the actors who were simply doing a job, and how it rocked everything he believed about who he was and what his life consisted of. The revelation shook his sense of self to the core, as if his world had just tumbled into the sea, leaving him adrift in confusion. I thought of his sense of sadness, anger, fear, deception, and betrayal.

And I understood exactly.

For several long moments, Mum, George, Kathy, and I tried processing this rattling loop of emotion. My not saying anything was, in itself, a miracle to anyone who knew me. I could feel my family's eyes fixed on me for my reaction. They were waiting for it.

Finally, I managed a single question, one that for me was of the utmost importance. "Am I still Greek?" I had been picked on so much by the neighborhood kids, when I was growing up, for being an ethnic minority and from an immigrant family that I just had to know whether it had all been warranted or I had suffered needlessly!

George, Kathy, and Mum burst out laughing. I couldn't help but join them. We so needed that laughter to de-intensify the moment. It had been such a hard, long afternoon, full of one shocking revelation after another. With its first burst, the laughter relieved the tension. And it did something more. It ushered back some of our familiar trust, our unquestioned love for one another, and with that, one more revelation.

THE THINGS I KNEW FOR SURE

As it all began to sink in that so much of what I thought to be true about my life was a lie, a surprising thing happened. Instead of being shattered, I felt an assurance rise within me.

True, I had just discovered that I wasn't who I thought I was. I had no idea who my biological parents were, and I knew nothing about them. I didn't know if I had been conceived out of love, a careless one-night stand, an affair, or a rape. When my birth mother gave me up for adoption, was she reluctant about it? Did she feel forced? Or was she eager to be rid of the inconvenience? I didn't know whether she and my birth father loved each other or had stayed together. Did he even know that I existed? Were they still alive? Why had she never contacted me? Did I have other brothers and sisters somewhere?

There was so much I didn't know. I was amazed that so many questions can flood your mind in a split second as it races from one thought to the next.

And yet.

Despite all that, there was also so much I knew for sure. So much that nothing my mum had said, nothing she could possibly say, would turn into a lie.

NOTHING SEPARATES US FROM GOD'S LOVE

Without thinking about what I was doing, I stood to my feet, looked at George, then Kathy, then Mum, and proclaimed with undaunted conviction, "Before I was formed in my mother's womb"—and here I paused to add, unable to resist, "whosever's womb that was"—"God knew me. He knitted together my innermost parts and fashioned all of my days before there was even one of them. I am fearfully and wonderfully made.[1] Even though I've only just found out that I was adopted, God has always known, and he has always loved me. And since *that* has never changed, therefore essentially *nothing* has changed. I may not be who I thought I was, but I still am who he says I am. And I am more. I am loved. I am his."

Mum, George, and Kathy just stared at me.

I stared back. They seemed as shocked by my words as by the news about the adoptions. I was a little shocked myself. Even as the underpinnings of my world had shifted radically, they were resettling in a more secure place. Even as things seemed to be falling apart, the truth of God's love was holding me together. And that truth was that I knew he loved me, unquestionably, unconditionally, whether I was adopted or not. The truth was that his love is relentless, unyielding, passionate, unfailing, perfect. A feeling of peace, supernatural peace, engulfed me. I was okay. Everything was going to be okay. That may seem like an odd conclusion, considering that my life, or at least everything I thought I knew about my life, was unraveling before my eyes. Nevertheless, I felt undaunted by it all, because of an unchanging, never-failing truth, a truth I clung to tenaciously: God was in control of my life, and I trusted him. He knew this day would come, and he was already in it, ready to meet me in it when I finally arrived. He knew the end from the beginning, and he had a plan for my life, regardless of how my start in life began.[2]

Of course, I thought, *nothing like a few quakes to test that belief. But do I really believe God is who he says he is?*

Yes. I did. God's promises were real, including the one where he told me, I love you. Nothing can separate you from my love. Nothing can take you from me.[3]

Mum and George and Kathy must have wondered, *In the face of all that has been unleashed this afternoon, how can you possibly feel such peace and positivity and resolve?*

It may have seemed a miracle, but it wasn't a mystery.

THE TRUTH SETS US FREE

For more than a decade, I had immersed myself daily in God's Word. I had memorized countless verses about God's love for me. I desperately needed his love, and when I read how he loved me, how he had a place for me, I soaked it up.[4] I meditated on those words, pondered and prayed over them. I found life in them. I found courage in them. The words contained promises that excited me so much that I began to preach them. I told myself and others about the unconditional love of God, how each one of us is created by him and for him and for a purpose.[5] I shared how God never leaves us nor forsakes us, that he is always with us in every circumstance, that his right hand upholds us, that he is our very present help in time of need.[6]

Now those promises were holding me. What Jesus promised was real: When you believe God is who he says he is, when you hang onto him and his Word in faith, his truth sets you free.[7] The truth you store up in silence comes back to you in the storm, and it lifts you away as on a life raft from the fears and disappointments that would otherwise pull you under. When you abide in his Word, he abides in you.[8] You find the strength to live undaunted.

Despite the day's unsettling revelations, I could feel the unconditional love of my heavenly Father engulf me even as I sat there with my family. The truth was and still is that I had been adopted into God's family when I surrendered my life to Christ. Christ was my brother, and God my Father. I needn't be unsettled by the thought of adoption, because I'd already been adopted by God![9] I was his child. And he loved me and promised to always love me and be right beside me in any situation, even this one.

WE WERE LOVED BEFORE
WE WERE EVEN BORN

Mum smiled at me with wonder and relief. Though I had been shaken by everything that afternoon, I hadn't been shaken *loose*. I wasn't melting down.

My calm gave Mum a glimpse into the power of God's love, and that glimpse gave her courage. She told me about the spring day the hospital called her with the news that I'd been born. Mum had been at the neighbor's, visiting over cups of tea in the back yard. So my grandmother, who had answered the phone, shouted over the neighbor's fence, "We have a girl! We have a girl!"

"I loved you," Mum said. "I loved you before I even met you."

Hearing that from her was like hearing the truth that had brought me to my feet just a moment ago, like hearing an echo of Psalm 139:13–16:

You created my inmost being;
 you knit me together in my mother's womb.
I praise you because I am fearfully and wonderfully made;
 your works are wonderful,
 I know that full well.
My frame was not hidden from you
 when I was made in the secret place,
 when I was woven together in the depths of the earth.
Your eyes saw my unformed body;
 all the days ordained for me were written in your book
 before one of them came to be.

God knew me and loved me before I was even me. He knew me before I was born and throughout my adoption, and he knew me even now that I wasn't sure who I was anymore. He loved me despite any trouble I found myself in or challenges I faced. I could mess up or melt down and he would love me still. He knew me so much better than I knew myself, and he loved me so much that he would always have my back in any challenge or distress, even go before me through anything unknown.

Yes, I thought. *I'm not who I thought I was. I am so much more. I am loved by God, the maker of the universe, the maker of me, and I was loved by him before I was born and will be after I die.*

LOVE WILL CARRY YOU

Mum, George, Kathy, and I were spent. We hugged our goodbyes, knowing we needed time and space to process the day's events. We'd withstood as much emotional earthquake as each of us could bear for one day.

I suddenly longed for some normality. Routine. I decided to keep a meeting that was scheduled back at the office. I felt that would help me find and keep my footing.

On the drive back to work, I called our younger brother Andrew (he's biological!) and gave him a quick version of all that had happened. "I'll tell you more later," I said. I was going to have to hurry if I wanted to get to the office in time. Besides, I needed some silence, some think time.

I got off the phone and let myself relax into the instinctive rhythm of driving. I rolled down the windows and felt the breeze sweep my face, brushing my wisps of hair straight back. I rested in the comfort of finding my way through my favorite neighborhoods, passing buildings and houses that had stood for decades, and listening to the consistent hum of the tires on the pavement. The simplistic familiarity soothed my heart as much as it did my senses, as did God's faithful assurances.

I knew that God cherishes us, because his steadfast love for us is abounding. He is faithful, and his love for us never ends. He lavishes his love on us, calling us the children of God.[10]

I knew that he claims us, because he has even written our names on the palms of his hands. He's recorded them in heaven, in the Book of Life.[11]

I knew that he carries us, because he promised that "even to your old age and gray hairs . . . I am he who will sustain you. I have made you and I will carry you . . . I will rescue you."[12]

Calmed by those thoughts, I was emotionally drained but strangely at peace. The truth that I'd known all those years seemed real to me in a new way: I'd been adopted by God long before I was adopted by Mum and Dad, and he cherishes me, claims me, carries me.

That is just what love does, I thought. *It cherishes us and claims us and carries us.*

Though Mum didn't carry George or me in her womb, love helped her carry the secrets of our births over all these years because she wanted to protect us.

When I arrived at the office, I walked in feeling almost lighthearted. The meeting I planned to join had already started. Sitting down, I looked around the room at the faces of my colleagues.

Together we were committed to bringing God's love and his promises to kids with eating disorders, kids who harmed themselves, kids who were marginalized and from broken families and in gangs, kids looking for love and a place to belong, to be cherished and claimed and carried.

Though I hadn't planned on it, when I saw their faces, I decided to share with my team what had just happened. They needed to see how Jesus is the anchor of our souls no matter what we face.[13]

"You're not going to believe this," I began, and when I finished telling them about the revelations of the day, the shock that I had felt hours earlier clearly registered on their faces.

"Are you okay?"

"Why didn't your parents ever tell you?"

"And you never had a clue?"

Then a question I hadn't expected, that I hadn't yet asked myself. "What are you going to do?"

WHAT ARE YOU GOING TO DO?

Life will eventually turn every person upside down and inside out. No one is immune. Not the mom who finds out her teen daughter is pregnant. Not the husband who is entangled in a financial disaster. Not the kid whose parents are strung out on drugs. Not the girl enslaved in human trafficking. Not the boy who's hungry and without any prospect of enough to eat.

And not the woman who finds out her whole sense of identity is based on a family connection that turns out to be a lie.

Not you.

Not me.

But just as life will upend you, so will love.

Love has the power to undo you for fear of losing it, as it did my parents over the thought of George and me discovering our adoption. Love has the power to bewilder, as it does when a baby, a new life, comes into your world.

God's love, which knows you and claimed you before you were even born, can take you beyond yourself, as it did Jesus, who left heaven to go to the cross and pass through the grave in order to bring us back home. God's love can bring you through emotional earthquakes, as it did me the afternoon I was told news that could have flattened me, but instead I was carried by God's promises. Love like God's can lift you out of betrayal and hurt. It can deliver you from any mess. Love like that can release you from every prison of fear and confusion. And love like God's can fill you up till it spills out of you, and you have to speak about it and spread it around.

"What are you going to do?" my coworkers asked. Well, I had definitely been affected by the news of my adoption. Despite my resolute—or perhaps desperate—clinging to God's Word and his promises, I would have been something other than human if I hadn't been emotionally stunned by what I'd learned that day. But I was not going to allow myself to be daunted by it. I couldn't. In the years I had been serving the Lord with all my heart, I had watched so many people allow life-changing news like this to drive them into anger, resentment, and depression, to push them to question their identity and self-worth and value. I knew how daunting this news could be if I did not choose, on that day and for all the days ahead, to bring each of my thoughts and feelings into compliance with what I knew of God. I chose to trust that, in ways I could not yet see, God would use this. God would not only uphold me as I worked through it but also honor the process of my journey by pointing out ways in which this unexpected and life-changing revelation could be used for his glory. I had no idea yet what those ways would be, but I had faith that they would come, that a calling would emerge.

What was I going to do?

As I pondered my team's question, my thoughts turned from my own concerns to those of others, to everyone our group had been called to serve.

Love. That's what I'm going to do. I am going to love others like I never have before.

Chapter 3

NUMBER 2508
OF 1966

———∞———

I was home alone, preparing a meal, when the doorbell rang. With my fingers still dripping with lemon juice that I'd squeezed onto chicken to marinate for the night's barbecue, I ran for the door, wiping my hands on a towel as I went.

Opening the door, I found the postman smiling at me. "Mrs. Christine Caine?"

"That would be me."

"I have a registered envelope here for you. I just need your signature."

"Sure," I said absentmindedly, still thinking of all I had to do in the kitchen. "Where do I sign?"

He pointed to a line, where I scribbled my name, staining his receipt book with a smear of lemon juice. I smiled apologetically and took the envelope from his hand.

It had been quite a while since I had signed for anything, even at the office, where most of our business correspondence went. *Who is sending registered mail to my home address?* I scanned the official envelope, which had my name and address typed front and center.

The upper left corner imprint read, "Department of Community Services." Even though I had been expecting it to arrive someday, my heart still skipped a beat.

It's here. Just weeks ago, after a full year of wrestling with whether to do this, I'd written to the Department of Community Services, asking for all the information available about my adoption. The decision to make the request had been torture. For months I had agonized over so many questions. *Who are my biological mother and father? Where are they now? Do I look like them? Do I want to know more about them? Does God want me to know? How would it make Mum feel?* I didn't want to hurt her, but below the surface so many questions simmered—a natural curiosity I couldn't seem to quench. I had decided to take it one step at a time. I would write to get the information. After that, I would decide whether to pursue anything further.

Still, standing there in the foyer, I realized I might be holding the answers to all my questions. I fingered the edges of the envelope, thinking how thin it seemed for something so monumental in my life. For a few moments, my fingers twitched a little, torn between ripping the envelope open or waiting. *No,* I decided finally, running a finger along the seal. *Not just yet.* I walked back to the kitchen, gently placing the mail on the dining table as I passed.

At least a dozen times as I kept preparing dinner, I found myself staring across the room at it. *Why not just go open it? Why am I so hesitant to read what's inside? What am I so afraid of, anyway?* Once again, questions looped over and again in my mind until, finally, I realized the heart of the issue. Even though I knew God loved me passionately, I had no idea what my biological mother and father thought of me. If they thought of me at all. *Why did they put me up for adoption? Do I really want to know? What if I don't like the answer?*

"This is ridiculous," I said, staring at the potatoes. I put down my knife, and with all the courage I had mustered, walked to the dining table, wiping my hands on my jeans. *Here goes.* I took a deep breath, sat in one of the chairs, and ripped open the seal.

The first piece of paper on the slim stack inside read, "Particulars of Child Prior to Adoption." I reread the title.

"Particulars of Child Prior to Adoption." Then I reread it again. And again. And once more.

Scanning the rest of the page, my eyes stopped when I read my biological mother's first name for the first time.

Panagiota.

I stared, my eyes unable to move beyond it. *Panagiota. Pah-nah-YAW-tah.* I reread it and pronounced it in my head over and over again. *Panagiota.* One of the most common first names for a Greek woman, derived from the name of the Virgin Mary, a name that means holy, complete. *So I am Greek, after all.*

UNNAMED

Reading her name shocked me as much as hearing for the first time that I was adopted. For a full year, I had known that there was a woman out there who'd given birth to me. But to see her name, a name other than Mum's, whose name I had printed on every legal document for my entire life—for more than thirty years—stopped me cold with a force I hadn't expected. Suddenly, in my heart, and not just in my head, Panagiota was real. She was more than a name in a tiny box on a legal document, more than the shadowy, ghostly, faceless figure of "birth mother" that I'd carried in my mind for the past year. She was a whole person with a real life—someone with an entire history that was part, though a hidden part, of my own story.

I wondered what she looked like. *Do I resemble her? Was she young when she had me? Older? Does she like moussaka or fish and chips? Greek music or English? Movies? And what kind? Comedies? Thrillers? When she was just a girl, did she wander off in stores, as I had from the aisles of dolls to the section filled with books? After school, did she make her way to the soccer fields for a game with the boys instead of practicing ballet with the girls?* I thought of all the things that had set me apart from my family when I was growing up, things that had seemed a mystery to them—and to me. What if those things had been Panagiota's style, her way—simply *her*. What if I had been like her?

Now that I knew her name, my research was no longer just about me. I could no longer think only of myself. Now I thought of her as well—Panagiota. *What questions might you want to ask me? What happened to you? What has your life been like? Do you ever think of me? Did you ever tell anyone that I exist?*

For a long while I sat, stunned by the difference it made to know her name. Panagiota had at one time been just a girl, her whole life ahead of her, with no idea she would one day give birth to a girl, a daughter whom she would give away. And yet, though she did give me up, we were still part of one another, and there was so much more I wanted to know beyond what her first name could tell me.

I read on.

Below the box with her name was another box, this one marked, "Father's Name." I took a deep breath. Inside that box was typed just a dash. He had no name. He was unknown to the authorities. To the hospital. To the doctors and nurses. And to me. They might as well have typed, "Unknown."

I lingered over this box, trying to understand how someone so critical to my existence and so important to me could be completely anonymous. Why hadn't Panagiota told them his name?

Somewhere, somehow, more than thirty years ago, my biological father came together with Panagiota to conceive a child, and the only record of his involvement with her, with me, was a dash.

I know more about my dentist, whom I see once a year, I thought, *than I may ever know about the man who is my biological father.*

Then my eyes moved to the next line. In an instant, I froze, and it felt like all the air was sucked out of the room. I could have sworn someone kicked me in the gut. I struggled to breathe. To grab onto something stable inside. Was I seeing correctly? Was I reading this right? In a box marked, "Child's Name" was a single word printed in big, bold, black, typewritten strokes. Seven letters: "Unnamed."

UNKNOWN AND UNWANTED

It's said that the punch that knocks you out is the one you never saw coming—and that's certainly how I felt about being labeled unnamed. I felt blindsided, the wind knocked out of me. I'd had many conversations over the past year with my close friends about my adoption and the circumstances surrounding my birth. How many times had I mused aloud with them? *Did my biological parents know each other? Did they love each other? Was I an accident in the heat of one night's passion? Maybe they weren't equipped to handle a baby and thought it best for me to go to a couple with resources, with know-how, with experience. Maybe they felt forced by their situation.* I even prepared myself to accept the possibility that my biological mother and father—if he were even still in the picture—just didn't want me.

Yet in all my conversations, never once had I questioned who I was at my core. Never once did I question the very essence of my being in God. My identity was in Christ. I knew that. *Whatever they think of me,* I'd resolved, *God loves me.*

But now one short word mocked me. *Unnamed? I was unnamed until adopted? No one even cared enough to give me a name?*

I could no longer hold back the tears burning my eyes. Helplessly spilling over, they streamed down my face as the document taunted me. *You weren't important enough to name.*

Worse, beneath that seven-letter word, something else reinforced my shock: a number.

I wasn't just unnamed. I was number 2508 of 1966.

What? I felt like I was having an out-of-body experience. I saw myself holding that paper, the official record of my entry to planet Earth, and on that paper I was described like something off a production line. Like an airline flight, a car, a zip code, a digit on a calculator, a safety deposit box, or some other inanimate object or sequence. That nameless, faceless number could represent anything. Yet here, right on this piece of paper, number 2508 represented me. I was nothing more than a number.

But suddenly everything in me screamed otherwise. I wanted to shout, *I have a name! I am a person! I am Christine, a human being, created in the image of God himself, with a calling to fulfill, a person filled with his purpose.*[1] *I am the girl who once hoped to play table tennis for Australia in the Olympic Games, the woman who relishes chick flicks while eating popcorn with salt and butter, who loves reading, who craves dark chocolate–covered licorice.*

How could number 2508 reflect that I was a real, living, breathing person with likes and passions, aversions and fears, hopes and dreams?

I sat immobile a long time, staring through a blur of tears at the official record of my birth:

UNNAMED
NUMBER 2508 OF 1966

Air, I thought suddenly. *I need air. And caffeine.*

I forced myself to stand and walk back to the kitchen to brew an extra-strong cup of coffee, and all my questions followed me. *How could you carry a child for nine months, feel the heartbeat and the twists and turns inside you, go through labor, and then, after all that, not have some name for this little being, this new life, this part of you to whom you gave birth?* In my heartbroken state, I couldn't imagine a single plausible answer.

Glancing at the clock, I was jarred back to reality. Dinner!

Quickly cutting up the last of the vegetables, I placed them in a dish, put them in the oven, and set the timer. Pouring my coffee and taking a sip to steady myself, I looked heavenward and prayed, "God, help me handle this." Then I grabbed my Bible and the adoption papers and headed to the couch in the living room. If I was going to face any more earthshaking facts, I'd do it with his Word in hand and with prayer.

I pulled the next piece of paper from the stack—an extract from Panagiota's hospital records, a partial transcript of her meeting with the social worker two weeks before I was born.

Why only a portion? I wondered. *Why wasn't I sent the entire document?*

I started to read, frustrated not only by the scant information but also by the clinical, medical tone. "Her estimated date of confinement is the third of October and she plans to give the baby away on adoption. She does not seem to be too emotionally involved with the child. She seems to want to get it all over with and get back to work as soon as possible."

Not emotionally involved with the child? Wants to get it all over with and get back to work? The words threw another swift punch. I could feel the room begin to spin. The emotional blow was so real, so strong, that it might as well have been physical.

My mind raced. *This is what I am. Unnamed, from an unknown man, and unwanted, and I have the legal documents to prove it.* The idea of such proof hurt more than anything else. Having no name, I decided, was just as bad as being called something horrible: worthless, failure, flawed, defective, deficient—and on the list grew, to at least a dozen more negative labels.

Even though I knew by heart God's promise that I was his creation, intended for good works, and that God even planned those good works in advance[2]—whatever they were—these words struck me like one jab after another, determined to knock me out:

FROM UNKNOWN
UNNAMED
NUMBER 2508 OF 1966
UNWANTED

Strangely, at the same time, I was rational enough to fight back, to tell myself that the word *unwanted* appeared nowhere on the record. I reread it, aloud this time. "She seems to want to get it all over with and get back to work as soon as possible."

But fight as I may, I couldn't ignore how the report made me feel. *What else could that mean but unwanted?* I scanned the two pages again—the "particulars" page, the excerpt of the interview with my biological mother. Together, to me, they shouted unworthy, incomplete, undesirable, unlovable. Unwanted. Unchosen.

GOD ALWAYS KNEW MY NAME

Isn't it strange how in times of doubt and dismay, we calculate things so desperately? We see or hear things and add them up incorrectly, perhaps based on our perceptions. We choose to believe what may be *somewhat* factual but simply isn't true. We accept what someone else has said and then conclude something false about ourselves.

Why is it always so hard to choose first what God says about us? Why do we listen to the voices of others more than his? If our goal is to be undaunted, then we should be especially diligent to not let the lies and foolish thoughts of others daunt us. Labels, insults, attempts to overwhelm and limit and thereby control us—these have no place in the life of the believer. God has freed us, and if we're to live undaunted, we can't allow the maneuvering of others to force us back into bondage.

But it is a fight, the good fight of faith.[3]

As I held that paper in my hand and stared at those words, I felt a nudge in my heart that I knew came from God. *Open my Word to Isaiah 49.* His voice was as clear and familiar as my own. It was certain, soothing, strong. He was going to help me fight. I smiled for the first time since I'd closed the front door to the postman.

I may not know who my biological father is, I thought, *but I do know who my heavenly Father is. I know his voice when I hear it.* And because of that, before I even turned the pages of my Bible, I knew I was going to be okay. I was hearing my Father's voice. He was with me. He was fulfilling his promise to me that he would never leave me nor forsake me, even when it felt like others had abandoned me.[4]

I found the book of Isaiah, turned to chapter 49, and began to read at verse 1. "Listen, O coastlands, to Me, and take heed, you peoples from afar!"[5]

God was speaking directly to me! I was sitting in my house in Sydney, Australia, a large island with plenty of coastlands, and being Down Under, I was definitely among a people from afar. *Okay,* I thought. *You have my attention, Father.*

"The LORD has called Me from the womb."[6]

The verse warmed and calmed me. I was not an accident. I was not unwanted. I was not unchosen. God had called me. He had not left me out, had not overlooked me, had not chosen instead someone more gifted, more talented, better looking, or smarter. He had called me from the womb, before I even arrived on the delivery table. He had a purpose for my existence, for all the years of my life.

"From the matrix of My mother He has made mention of My name."[7]

I gasped. As stunned as I'd been when I read the word *unnamed,* this idea struck me even more deeply. This was the truth I needed to anchor my heart. *God called me by name while I was still inside my mother. God named me before this document stamped me as unnamed. Before I became a number, I had a name. I have always had a name. Yes!*

I laughed. I was chosen before I was even formed in my mother's womb. All the details about who I was and who I would be were determined before I began to take shape: my eye color and shoe size, the curve of my smile, the length of my legs. God shaped my body and my spirit. He created the sound of my voice and the loop of my penmanship, the strength of my grip and the capacities of my mind.

I couldn't take my eyes off the phrase: "From the matrix of My mother He has made mention of My name."

I felt the Lord speaking so clearly to me. *Your birth certificate may say you're unnamed, but I named you when you still were in your mother's womb. You aren't a number to me. You aren't unnamed. I knew before you were born that you would be adopted and that your adoptive parents would name you Christine. I have chosen you for great things. These documents in front of you don't define you or your destiny. My Word is the final authority on that. And I formed you. Your freedom will be determined by whether you allow what I think and say about you to matter more than what anyone else thinks or says, including your biological mother or workers filling out forms for the Department of Community Services. They have said what you are not. But I say what you are, who you are, and you are created in my image, not theirs. You reflect my glory.*

I breathed deeply and exhaled. It was as though God's words were clearing the air and burning away the fog.

I lifted my Bible in one hand and with my other scooped up all the documents regarding my adoption, including the particulars of my birth. Both hands held paper that contained words printed in black ink. Both contained facts. Yet only one held the truth. I knew that to move forward, I had to choose which of these documents I would entrust with my life.

The choice was clear.

TRUTH PREVAILS OVER FACTS

We can allow the names we call ourselves to define us. We can allow the labels that others place on us to define us. After all, from the time we're born, and then throughout life, our personal characteristics are often typed into boxes—on birth certificates, on driver's licenses, job applications, marriage licenses, loan applications, and eventually on death certificates. We're defined in little boxes on forms by our family of origin, address, education, experience, bank account, credit score, employer, friends, race, and ethnicity. We're labeled one thing or another: educated or uneducated, responsible or reckless, qualified or inexperienced, young or old, shy or outgoing, too much or not enough. We can allow those words and labels to limit us. A teacher, parent, colleague, or ex can call us loser, fat, ugly, or hopeless, and those labels can stick to us, hurt us, and damage us because we begin to believe them.

Remember that old adage from our childhoods, "Sticks and stones can break my bones, but names will never hurt me"? That thought may help us keep a resilient will and a stiff upper lip, but we know from experience it's not a truthful statement, especially when it comes to our hearts. We can be hurt plenty by names: stupid, ignorant, alcoholic, addict, criminal, weak, pitiful. Names like these can break our spirits as much as sticks and stones can bruise and bloody our bodies, especially if we believe them and begin to use them on ourselves. They can bring us to our knees, stop us in our tracks before we even get started in life. Even when those names reveal something true about us, they are at best a partial truth, as well as a misleading one. If we allow them to loom larger in our hearts and minds than the promises of God, they can fool us into missing God's truth about who we are and what we were created to do, so that we don't pursue the purpose God has had in mind for us from the beginning of time.

When there is a fight between our hearts and our heads, experience has taught me that the best thing we can do is pick up our Bible and remind ourselves of what God says. Our heads can insist that God created us and loves us, but our hearts and emotions may keep fighting against that knowledge with condemning punches like, *What's wrong with me? I never seem to do anything right!* Those kinds of blows can give us an overwhelming sense of worthlessness and rejection, because that is what untruth about ourselves does. It beats us down and knocks us out.

If we want to find peace, then we need to do what I did that day. We need to return to the truth of God's Word that will last forever, not meditate on circumstances that will change and fade.[8]

It is this truth that enables us to move forward into the future undaunted.

GOD CALLS EACH OF US BY NAME

The truth I clung to that day saved me, like it has so many times: I was not an accident. I am not unknown, unnamed, or unwanted. And neither are you.

I understand that every baby arrives on the planet differently. Some are loved, prayed over, and planned for by conscientious parents.

Others are surprises who are wanted or unwanted. Some are conceived in love, while others are conceived by force. Some are born prematurely. Some breech. Some are delivered by C-section, and others are pushed out in a few minutes. Some are brought home to beautifully decorated nurseries, heirloom cribs, and plush rockers. Others get hand-me-downs or nothing at all.

Like me, some of us may not like or know the circumstances of our birth, but not one of us needs to be defined by or limited by our start in life. Each of us has the opportunity to be born again in Christ, to experience a second birth, and to connect with our eternal purpose.[9] Our beginning never needs to define our purpose, our identity, or even our destiny.

God says we were designed and made to do good works in Christ, works prepared before the creation of the world.[10] So no matter how we were born, no matter the particulars of our birth, we each were chosen in eternity long before we ever arrived at this point in time. If God created us to do good works of eternal significance, then he would not create us ill-prepared. Let these truths settle our hearts:

- *God made each one of us.* We may not know what our parents felt for each other, or even if they knew each other, when we were conceived, but each of us is God's workmanship, not the workmanship of anyone else. "We are God's handiwork, created in Christ Jesus to do good works, which God prepared in advance for us to do."[11] We are each a masterpiece, made intricately and lovingly by his own hands. It is *that*—not the identity of our parents—which gives us our identity.
- *He names us.* Before we were given a name by our earthly parents, God already knew us, and he called us. "I have redeemed you; I have called you by your name."[12] He's even carved our names in the palms of his hands. "Can a mother forget the baby at her breast and have no compassion on the child she has borne? Though she may forget, I will not forget you! See, I have engraved you on the palms of my hands."[13]

- *God chooses each one of us.* None of us is an afterthought or an accident. My adoption papers may have identified me only as a number, just another in a series of births, but God *selected* me individually. He designed me in eternity, designed me to be with him beyond the trappings of time, and he selected you in this way too. You are chosen. "You are a chosen people, a royal priesthood, a holy nation, God's special possession, that you may declare the praises of him who called you out of darkness into his wonderful light."[14] This is wonderful news for those of us rejected by society for reasons of race, gender, education, or social status or for any other difference. Society sometimes makes it clear that we are not valued at all, but can that matter when the Creator of the universe has chosen us, individually, by name, for a great mission he would entrust to no one else?

- *He saves us.* Like me, you may have been given away by your biological parents, but God has made a way for each of us to be born again. Think of it as a do-over. He wipes away the mess of our past and gives us a brand-new start and a hope for the future, and he promises that to each of us, always. "If anyone is in Christ, he is a new creation; old things have passed away; behold, all things have become new."[15]

- *God is always with us.* Even if our parents discard us, God will never leave us. He promises: "Be strong and courageous. Do not be afraid or terrified because of them, for the LORD your God goes with you; he will never leave you nor forsake you."[16] Whatever circumstances we encounter, or wherever we may be, God is always there with us, beside us, around us, and within us.

- *He is our Father.* I may never meet my biological dad, this unknown man listed as a dash on the paperwork I received. I may never know what he looked like and what things he liked. You may not know your parents either. But we do know the one who has made himself known to us—our Abba Father. "The Spirit you received does not make you slaves, so that you live in fear again; rather, the Spirit you received brought about your adoption to sonship. And by him we cry, 'Abba, Father.'"[17] Our heavenly Father promises that we can know his voice and that we will become more like him every day.[18]

Regardless of what our parents may or may not have planned or intended, from God's perspective there was nothing accidental or unintentional about my birth or yours.

Yes, there are things in our lives, God tells us, that we will not understand.[19] But he knows. He always knows. And if we're to live successfully, if we're to live undaunted, then we must learn to trust that his thoughts are higher than our thoughts, and his ways are higher than our ways.[20] That he knows all things.[21]

Most of the time, when we humans choose, we choose exclusively, meaning we select something and exclude everything or everyone else. A starting lineup may be picked for the game, while other players remain on the bench. An intern may be chosen for a job, while another candidate will need to wait for her chance. Yet God chooses everyone, all the time, and he chose each of us first.[22] He never chooses one person at the exclusion of another. He loves each one of us so much that he paid the price for every person to be forgiven and reconciled to him.

WE ARE HIS CALLED AND CHOSEN ONES

That day—the day I learned I was unwanted, unnamed, and the daughter of a man who would remain forever unknown to me—could have devastated me. And for a moment it did, until God reminded me that his word means more than anyone else's.

Since that day, I've spoken about my birth and adoption openly and often. I've shared with others how my true identity is in Christ, how God has chosen me and called me by name. As I have, people have shared with me their own adoption stories.

Some women have sobbed gut-wrenchingly over children they

gave up for adoption, feeling overwhelmed by guilt and loss. Others have told me how they learned they were adopted, and how afterward they struggled with a deep sense of rejection and lack of identity. Other women have shared with me how they chose abortion and carry guilt and shame, sadness and remorse.

I had no idea that my story would connect with so many people and so many circumstances. But with every conversation, with every prayer, with every tear shed over all sides of this issue of adoption, I realized that because I knew, despite my past, that I was chosen by God, I could help others discover that they too had been chosen by God and for God, whatever the circumstances of their lives. Because we know that we're chosen, because we've heard God call our names, we can help others hear God call their names and find great peace and great purpose.

The truth is that nothing about my birth—or yours—was random or accidental. I was born for this time, and so were you. We were each chosen for a particular, cosmically important purpose. Therefore let's be diligent in listening to God's voice leading us in discovering that purpose and in encouraging others to recognize that God has a purpose for them as well.

Let's encourage the grocery clerk at the checkout stand and the downcast person we pass on the street. Let's recognize their value and call out their worth. Let's care enough to help the mom with preschoolers know that she won't feel overwhelmed forever. Let's love enough to offer a word of cheer or humor to the receptionist at the doctor's office struggling to answer phones and still respond to every question at the counter. Let's help others know they matter and tell them how much God loves every single one of us.

And let's especially remember that empowering others starts with believing that God loves and chooses us—always.

DO YOU HEAR IT?

Several months after the day I found out I was adopted, I asked Mum about the day she got the call from the hospital telling her that I had been born. How had she felt? What expectations had she had? It seemed I had as many questions for her as I did for Panagiota.

Her eyes lit up. Happy to share something joyful with me, she enthusiastically explained that she and Dad were desperately hoping for a girl, since they already had a son. But since there were no sonograms back then to reveal whether you were having a boy or a girl, they had to wait. Patiently. Mum was very close to her sister, who had four boys of her own and also hoped for a girl, so they would chat often about names and dreams for me.

One day my aunt suggested, "Why not Christine?"

"I like that," Mum said. And so the decision was made over a cup of tea. There was nothing deep or spiritual in their decision. They just both liked the name Christine.

I know that my name is derived from the Greek and Latin and means "Christ follower." And the Christ I follow has given me another name too—a name by which he calls me, a name by which he also calls you and so many others. It's a simple name. One word. Just four letters. Much like the word *love*. It resounds loudly through time and space because we have been chosen before time, born in his time, and destined to live throughout time.

He's even printed it in his book for us all to read, lest we ever forget: "Fear not, for I have redeemed you; I have called you by your name; you are Mine."[23]

Mine.

That's who he calls us. That's whose we are.

PART 2

GOD KNOWS MY PAIN

Chapter 4

HE HEALED MY HIDDEN WOUNDS

———— ∞∞∞ ————

I opened the door to find Nick on the doorstep with a dozen of the most beautiful roses I'd ever seen. Although we'd been dating for a year and I should have known him well by then, he still had this powerful way of impressing me. I loved that about him. He was truly the most thoughtful, kind, and generous man I had ever known, and he seemed to always find a way to make me feel so special. And best of all: lately, we'd been talking more about the future than about the present.

After quickly putting the roses in a vase of water, I grabbed my purse and we stepped outside. Nick opened the car door, and I got in, feeling my heart race a little faster, a little happier. I was looking forward to what I thought was on tap for the evening: dinner at our favorite Thai restaurant. As we drove off, we began chatting right away. I was so engrossed in our conversation that it was some time before I realized that we were in an unexpected part of the city, heading in the wrong direction. For the first time that evening, I paused.

"Nick?" I asked. "Are we lost?"

He smiled knowingly. "Just sit back and relax," he said. "I've got a surprise."

My heart began to race for totally different reasons. I felt overcome with a deep and sudden anxiety. *Where are we going? Why is Nick doing this? Doesn't he know I hate surprises?* I edged back in my seat, folded my arms, and braced every part of my being. There was no rational reason for me to feel as I did, to react the way I was reacting, but I couldn't help it. Mentally, I understood that Nick simply wanted to do something special. But emotionally, I couldn't shake the familiar dread, the suffocating fear, that surprises had triggered in me for as long as I could remember. I just didn't do surprises—ever.

I glanced over at Nick. I could tell from the way he'd set his jaw that he was frustrated by my less-than-enthusiastic demeanor. I couldn't blame him, but I felt helpless to control it. A minute later, he pulled over to the shoulder of the road, whipped a U-turn, and started driving back the way we'd come.

After a few minutes of tense silence, Nick slowed the car and turned to face me. "Christine," he said, eyes piercing and tone lowered, measuring each word, "this exact same thing keeps happening in so many different ways. I don't want to just ignore it. We need to talk, and we need to talk now. We're headed back to your place."

I swallowed hard. Nick had never spoken to me this way. It rattled me and made me feel even more anxious, because I'd upset him! And I definitely didn't want to explain to him why surprises always upended me. I tensed even more, dreading the conversation I'd spent most of my life avoiding.

Nick pulled into my driveway, slung the car in park, and wasted no time in getting to the point. He obviously wasn't going to wait until we were inside. "Christine, I'm on your side. I'm not trying to hurt you. But for some reason, anytime I try to do something spontaneous, or anytime it seems as if things are slipping out of your direct control, you freak out. Then if I try to talk to you about it, you put up walls and shut me out emotionally. I don't know what's going on, but it's clear that you don't trust me, and if this relationship isn't based on trust, then what are we doing?"

I knew he was right as soon as the words came out of his mouth. I loved him. I did. But I didn't trust him completely. It had nothing to do with his character or anything he'd done. I just didn't trust anyone completely. I simply couldn't.

In a softer tone, he added, "You know I love you. But I can't shake the feeling that you're waiting for me to do something to disappoint you or hurt you—which I inevitably will—so you can have an excuse to end this. I want this to work out between us, Christine, but I need you to trust me, or there's really no point in going any farther."

This was not the first time Nick had challenged my defensive posture. Throughout our relationship, Nick had chipped away at many of the defenses I'd used to keep others at arm's length—mostly simple things, like not allowing him to open doors for me or carry a box. Fiercely independent, I insisted on doing things for myself. Nick was the first person to ever stick around long enough to break through some of my defenses. His gentle persistence at doing and fixing things for me was a new experience, and gradually I gave in to his help. In the process, he won my heart—just not all of it. There was a huge piece I couldn't help but hang onto.

Now Nick was fighting for that piece too. He was calling me out of the fortress I'd built to protect myself. In my head, I understood that we couldn't move ahead as a couple if I didn't let him into my confidence, my trust. And I wanted to be more open and trusting. But there was a barrier to that openness, a barrier that I had no hope I could ever overcome, and I dreaded the thought of trying.

My heart continued to pound. My palms sweated. My tongue felt like lead wrapped in paper. I couldn't seem to form words and thought that if I tried, the only sound likely to come out would be a croak. I could take the easy way out—just jump out of the car and walk away. Keep the protection I'd built around my heart and soul. But if I did that, I would lose him. As I sat there, wavering,

I desperately debated what to do: Stay behind all my protective barriers and keep silent? Or reveal what I'd hidden behind them?

It wasn't a new dilemma. For months, I'd spent half the time wanting to share with Nick everything about my past, and the other half positive that I never wanted to mention it. *Isn't my past just the past? Do I really need to tell him? Haven't I already dealt with it? If I tell him, will he think it was my fault? Will he wonder why I've never said anything? Will he question why I didn't find a way to stop it sooner? Will he want someone untouched?*

All the hurt I'd hidden—yet still felt—for years welled up inside. I thought I had dealt with it, resolved it, put it to rest. But now those old wounds threatened to reopen at any moment.

I looked up at Nick, and that one look resolved my dilemma. Seeing the bewilderment on his face was like looking in a mirror and seeing all the confusion I'd seen on my own face for so many years. For both of our sakes, I had to bring it out of the darkness and into the light. I had to move forward, undaunted, trusting God more than anyone, including Nick.

I took a deep breath and started slowly. "I do love you. I *want* to trust you; it's just not that easy for me." *How to say it? How to tell?* I breathed deeply again and, sitting there in the driveway, began to tell him how I had been abused for many years as a girl, by several different men. When I said the word *abused*, I started to shake. Telling the man I loved what other men had done to me was the hardest thing I had ever done.

As I spoke, I couldn't look at Nick. I looked at the floorboard of the car and poured out what I'd kept secret for years, things that had become unspeakable. And once I'd breached the dam, there was no holding anything back. It came out in a flood. *If I'm going to lose you over this, Nick,* I thought, *then you may as well know it all.* All the hidden things came pouring out: places, incidents, memories I hadn't even realized I'd buried so deeply and forgotten. One memory led to another, unfolding a narration of horror that shocked us both.

Finally, I stopped. Nick had not once interrupted. I had not once looked up, and now I felt exposed, vulnerable, spent. And yet, though I know it sounds cliched, I also felt a great weight lifted off me. For the first time, I felt a freedom I hadn't even known I lacked.

UNEARTHING MY BURIED HEART

The die was cast. There was no going back. I could no longer run. The past had caught up with me, and God was using this man I loved dearly to force me to deal openly with all the dark secrets.

And they hadn't been secrets I'd kept just from the rest of the world. Even I had been amazed by my emotional response to reliving those years of abuse. It was clear that there was much I had not admitted to myself: that I was still afraid because of what had happened to me. I was deeply shamed by the abuse, and it was evident that I still felt so much guilt, though it was undeserved, as with any victim. My heart had been utterly broken and trampled.

I'd thought that the part I'd hung onto had been healed. But now I knew that it wasn't healed at all. I had simply put a small bandage over a gaping wound, hoping that it would stop the bleeding, that the wound would mend itself and go away. I said I loved God with my whole heart, only my heart wasn't whole. It was broken and bruised and in pieces. I had vowed to never let anyone ever again hurt, betray, use, or abuse me. I hadn't realized that by locking myself behind these walls I thought would protect me, I was also locking out love. Now, through Nick, God was helping me confront a question I'd not reckoned with: Why didn't I believe that the miracle God could work in other people's hearts couldn't be worked in mine as well?

"Oh, Nick," I said, "I so want to trust you, but at a certain point, I can't seem to help but pull back to protect myself. Those men who hurt me were supposed to be men I could trust. I *did* trust them. My family did too. But they didn't prove trustworthy. And when one of them would move out of my life, and there would be a period when the abuse would stop, I would let down my defenses, thinking I had a chance to start over. Then the abuse would start again, an endless cycle. I learned it was safer to keep up my guard all the time than to trust anyone even some of the time."

The walls were crumbling.

"I feel pulled apart inside," I confessed. "I want to give you the key to the innermost recesses of my heart, but I don't know where I last put it. The frustrating thing is, you won't go! I know it sounds strange, but if by holding you at arm's length and failing to trust you, I can influence you to leave, then I've proven that I'm really not worth staying with, and so I can just give up because there's no real hope. If you stay, I'm forced to ask myself, *Is there actually something in me that makes me worth your time and sacrifice?*"

Before I could say another word, Nick reached over and pulled me close, holding me for the longest time. "I'm so sorry that ever happened to you," he eventually said. "I'm just so sorry."

I sat there motionless in his arms, utterly drained and tenderly comforted. *Does his heart really hurt that much for me? Does he love me so much that he feels a part of my pain? Does he really wish that he could somehow make it all better?*

He had surprised me after all. Nick now knew about my past—my secrets and shame and guilt—and he wasn't pushing me away. Quite the opposite. He was pulling me closer. He still loved me. And knowing all that he now knew, he seemed to love me even more.

I felt a stirring inside. It was my fragmented and wounded heart beginning to flutter with life, starting to be restored in ways I'd never imagined. Clearly, through Nick's earthly love for me, God was showing me another glimpse of his great divine and unconditional love.

DELIVERED BUT NOT FREE

For many years, I had been wounded by abuse. All those years of pain had caused me to seal away a part of my heart and soul in what

I thought was a safe, protected place. Though I fiercely craved close relationships, I desperately feared them. I never wanted to be hurt again. I felt as though I were trapped in a relational no-man's-land with no hope of escape.

Perhaps you too have felt this way before, when:

- an overbearing boss crushed your spirit
- an unfaithful spouse betrayed your trust
- cruel friends trampled your heart with spiteful words
- insensitive parents stripped your confidence
- unthinking teachers called you stupid, squashing your self-worth
- rebellious children stomped all over you

Whatever happened, whatever our story, we know: abusers try to take our souls. Whatever the source of the attack on our bodies, souls, and spirits, the hurt stings and the damage goes deep. And the memories can inflict just as much harm again and again.

Many of us remember the exact moment of the damage—how the earth seemed to stop spinning, how our world came to a halt. We can't forget the sights, the smells, a song playing, what we wore, who else was there. These things freeze in our memories, and a part of us freezes with them, forever stuck in a place, unable to move on.

In that place, we may be delivered from our situations, but we are not free.

When Nick confronted me, it was all too true. Though I was no longer in bondage to my abusers every day, I had shuttered my heart. I didn't trust anyone, not even God. I kept God at a distance by giving him my time but not all of myself. I didn't trust him to take care of me, any more than I trusted Nick.

I couldn't forgive the men who hurt me, nor myself for being abused. Worse, I realized that I hadn't forgiven God. Where was he, after all, when I was a helpless child and those men laid hands on me? Why didn't he stop them?

Did I really think that? How could I compel others to love God with their whole hearts when I kept a part of my own from him? How could I move, undaunted, into an unknown future with a God I did not trust?

Although I was shocked by this revelation, God was not. Since he knows everything, he knew that if I was to be truly free, I needed to deal with this wound. He was able to heal me, but I had to choose his healing. If I was to be made whole, first I had to admit that I wasn't. I had to accept that I needed help. I needed to reach up to God, and out to others, as part of the healing process. Only then could I purely love others. Especially Nick.

STEPS TOWARD WHOLENESS
AND HEALING

It's hard for someone who is supposed to have it all together to admit that she needs help. But that's exactly what I had to do. Hurting people hurt other people. I was hurt, and because of that, I hurt Nick and who knows how many others. If I was to stop hurting and instead find wholeness and healing, then I needed to forgive those who had abused me. But I also needed to go farther: I needed to trust Nick, who loved me, and I needed healing in my relationship with God.

I grappled with this idea for weeks after Nick and I talked in the driveway.

Here I was teaching students how to trust God in their daily walk, and now I had to learn to do that myself at a whole new level.

My questions were so big that I took them to a counselor. Though the walls around my heart had been pounded, they were still standing. I would never be free from the haunting memories and old feelings of shame, self-condemnation, anger, bitterness, and mistrust until I determined to make new memories and embrace new feelings such as peace, kindness, and compassion.

The process of breaking free and walking in wholeness starts within. God tells us to bear with one another.[1] Bearing means there will be pain to endure. The healing process ahead of me would take the touch of God's hand, as well as deliberation and work, and no elixir I could sip or pill I could pop would take away that process.

Healing, for any of us, doesn't happen overnight. Even when Naaman, a valiant Old Testament army commander who was stricken by leprosy, sought a cure, he was told to dip seven times in the muddy Jordan River in order to be healed.[2] He couldn't go to a prettier river with cleaner waters and just dip once. He had to get in the Jordan and bathe there again and again and again—seven times. Such a clear picture of how healing is such a messy process, but a choice he had to make.

So it is for us. If we trust God with our broken and wounded hearts, then he will bring healing, restoration, and wholeness. He takes the weak, the marginalized, and the oppressed and makes all things new. What someone else would leave for broken, he sees as beautiful. He sees us beyond where we are; he sees us as who he created us to be. That's the pattern of God I see in his Word. It's the pattern I see in the story of the lame man who was begging at the temple gate. People had walked by him for years, giving him money or ignoring him, but when Peter and John walked by, God reached out to him, just like he was reaching out to me.

One day Peter and John were going up to the temple at the time of prayer—at three in the afternoon. Now a man who was lame from birth was being carried to the temple gate called Beautiful, where he was put every day to beg from those going into the temple courts. When he saw Peter and John about to enter, he asked them for money. Peter looked straight at him, as did John. Then Peter said, "Look at us!" So the man gave them his attention, expecting to get something from them.

Then Peter said, "Silver or gold I do not have, but what I do have I give you. In the name of Jesus Christ of Nazareth, walk." Taking him by the right hand, he helped him up, and

instantly the man's feet and ankles became strong. He jumped
to his feet and began to walk. Then he went with them into
the temple courts, walking and jumping, and praising God.
When all the people saw him walking and praising God, they
recognized him as the same man who used to sit begging at
the temple gate called Beautiful, and they were filled with
wonder and amazement at what had happened to him.[3]

The man who was begging had been lame from birth. When
other babies were taking their first steps, he did not. When other
kids were running and playing, he could not. When teenagers were
working alongside their parents, learning a trade, he could not. His
muscles would have been atrophied, his limbs shriveled, distorted.
Much like our souls are from the time we're wounded.

We know from this passage that he was dependent on others
to carry him from his home to the temple area, up fifteen steps to
the gate, and place him there in front of it. He was laid daily at the
temple gate. The routine was set, the plan was set, the system was
set, and everyone acted according to the expectation. When we
expect and accept that this is how things will always be, we build
our lives around daily rituals that enable and ensure the life we have
settled for.

Because of his condition, he was not allowed to enter beyond
the gate. He was ostracized, marginalized, discarded, and overlooked. He was someone society would have seen as ugly and labeled
undesirable. The people entering the temple to pray at three in the
afternoon would have noticed him—every single day.

God chose to put the story of someone like this—someone who
physically wasn't easy to look at—in his inspired and holy Word, and
the story took place in front of a gate called Beautiful. What irony.

That gate was a one of a kind. Unlike all the other gates around
the temple, which were plated in gold and silver, this one was made
of solid, brilliant Corinthian brass. It was magnificent and massive,
an unusual size of more than sixty feet wide, more than thirty feet

tall. Its weight was so great that it took twenty men to move it. It gleamed in the afternoon sun, outshining all the others. It was strategically placed between two courts. The first court, where everyone entered, was inside the wall surrounding the temple—the holy ground of the outer court. On the other side of the gate called Beautiful was the inner court—the place of prayer and worship, the place of the presence of God.

The lame man was doomed to stay there, sitting outside against the massive doors of the gate, sentenced to a life of brokenness, until Peter and John came along. Until God extended to him an invitation.

The lame man asked for money.

Peter responded, "Look at us!" He sought to dignify, value, and humanize this man by asking him to look at them.

And the man had the courage to look at them, to look up. To change his perspective from being low to the ground, staring at his misery, to looking heavenward, where healing and miracles come from.

"Silver or gold I do not have," Peter said, "but what I do have I give you. In the name of Jesus Christ of Nazareth, walk."

I love this story because it shows that we often overestimate what people can do for us and underestimate what God wants to do for us. The man asked for money. Peter offered him healing. The man wanted a short-term solution. Peter offered him what he really needed—not pocket change but a life change.

Isn't that like God? To take what is ugly and make it beautiful? To reach out to us right where we are, where we seemingly don't fit in, and heal us? To see beyond our crippled brokenness to all the potential he placed inside us?

When Peter told the lame man to get up and walk, the man obeyed. He made the effort to rise up. To move forward in faith. That's all God ever asks us to do.

"Instantly the man's feet and ankles became strong. He jumped to his feet and began to walk."

Then he stepped foot where he'd never been able to go before.

"He went with them into the temple courts, walking and jumping, and praising God."

God cherishes us in our brokenness, but he'll never leave us there. He sends people—like Peter and John, like Nick—to notice us and show us his unconditional love. And then, as he heals us, he uses us to touch others: "When all the people saw him walking and praising God, they recognized him as the same man who used to sit begging at the temple gate called Beautiful, and they were filled with wonder and amazement at what had happened to him."

When the people saw the man and recognized him, a crowd gathered. It became the perfect opportunity for Peter to preach, and the man was used as a witness unto the power and person of Jesus.[4]

Our healing is always for more than just us. It's for all the people on the other side of our obedience. When the man looked up, he obeyed, undaunted, and he was healed. The result: multitudes came to Christ.

Isn't this the same work God was doing in me? Isn't this what he wants to do in you? He wants to lead us all through the gate called Beautiful, right into his presence. To put us on the path to our destiny, to fulfilling our calling. To free us to live undaunted. So multitudes can be helped.

ACCEPT GOD'S INVITATION

We have to choose to heal, and trust that if we do what God, the Great Physician, asks, then there will be change, good results, strength, and wholeness. When we accept his invitation to be healed, it means he will help us:

- *Forgive every time we feel anger or mistrust or bitterness.* Instead of dwelling on the emotions that were eating me alive, I had to forgive. For years, I'd thought that forgiving meant that I was letting my abusers off the hook. But my refusal to forgive them was doing more damage to me than to them. Like the old adage goes, not forgiving is like ingesting poison and expecting it to kill someone else. Unforgiveness keeps us cowardly and stunted, isolated and alone, ugly and bitter. Daunted. Jesus said to forgive seventy times seven because no matter how much you forgive others, he has forgiven you even more.[5] When the anger returns, when the pain resurfaces, when we don't want to forgive again, we must remember how much God forgave us.

- *Stay in the present moment or think on the future* instead of rehearsing old injustices and letting your life revolve around the past. There's greater reward in replacing our negative thoughts with what is pure and noble and lovely now—and in the future.[6] But we have a hard time thinking that way. We naturally default to what's negative or in the past. I needed to stretch and strain my mind and heart "to take hold of that for which Christ Jesus took hold of me."[7] Christ took hold of me and you to give all of us a new destiny—to make a difference in this world for him. The only way we can claim that destiny is to let go of our past and look ahead to a heavenly future.[8]

- *Let others make their own choices, and let go of the illusion of control.* We often try to manipulate the circumstances and the people around us. We are not in control. God is. He is sovereign.[9] This meant I could allow Nick to make decisions without questioning every single one or feeling the need to control him. He could choose a restaurant without consulting me, even if it meant surprising me.

- *Stop trying to punish with anger and hate those who hurt us.* Instead we can let God deal with them. If we're building walls to protect ourselves, we're just keeping God and others out. We think we'll get back at someone through anger or by ignoring them, but God wants us to drop it. He knows we are hurt.[10] We don't have to deny our pain, but we have to let go of our need to pay back. God won't let things go. He will contend on our behalf, but most likely not how we would do it.[11] We have to trust that he's got our back.

- *Trust in God instead of ourselves.* I've read how God guided the Israelites to the promised land. I've read how he directed people like the wise men to Jesus. How he led so many—even the misguided, like Paul—all the way to the place of hope and eternal salvation. I've learned to trust that what God did for others, he will do for me, if only I trust him and follow his leading. If only I will lean into him and believe that he is trustworthy like he says. "Trust in the LORD with all your heart and lean not on your own understanding; in all your ways submit to him, and he will make your paths straight."[12] No matter what any of us have been through, no matter what was meant to do us harm, God can use it for our good and for the good of others. God is able to take the mess of our past and turn it into a message. He can take our trials and tests and turn them into a testimony. I love the words of Joseph, the Old Testament hero who was abused by his brothers and sold into slavery: "You intended to harm me, but God intended it for good to accomplish what is now being done, the saving of many lives."[13]

The enemy meant evil against me when those men abused me, just as he meant evil against me when I was left unnamed and unwanted at a hospital. But God took what was meant to harm me and turned it for my good. He healed me and taught me how to reach out to others so they can be healed too. Romans 8:28 does not say that all things that happen to us are good, but it does say that God is able to work all things together for the good of those who love him and are called according to his purpose.

MY PAST COULD GIVE
SOMEONE ELSE A FUTURE

Because I was willing—not necessarily able but willing—to take one step and then another and another, like when the lame man at the gate called Beautiful stood up, God has taken what I thought was broken and unworthy—my heart—and made it into something beautiful. Because of the healing he has done in me, I can help others who are flattened by life and circumstance.

He wants to do the same with you. Which of your mistakes and hurts can help give someone else a future? Trust me, God doesn't waste one experience of our lives. He uses everything to help someone else. He doesn't want us to remain crippled, immobilized, paralyzed by the past. Instead he sent Jesus to show us how to get up and walk and step into the future. Undaunted.

God chooses imperfect vessels, like me, like all of us who have been wounded, who have physical or emotional limitations. Then he prepares us to serve and sends us out with our weakness still in evidence, so that his strength can be made perfect in that weakness.[14] More often than not, it's our weakness that makes us capable of serving, because those we serve identify with our pain. It's as 2 Corinthians 1:3–4 says: "Praise be to the God and Father of our Lord Jesus Christ, the Father of compassion and the God of all comfort, who comforts us in all our troubles, so that we can comfort those in any trouble with the comfort we ourselves receive from God." As always, God works in us so that he can work through us.

I am so glad God used Nick to begin a process of healing and restoration in my heart. I never imagined that all the fears from my past that had paralyzed me for years could be used to give me such courage to live an undaunted life. But that is just what happened.

Months after our driveway conversation, Nick took me out for a surprise dinner, and true to form, I panicked. He took me to the Dining Room, a beautiful restaurant overlooking the harbor in Sydney, Australia, and asked me to marry him.

And then, not so surprisingly, my response was, "Are you asking me to marry you?" I was so overwhelmed, I told him I couldn't give him an answer right then and ran to the bathroom. I called my best friend, Kylie, and told her I was freaking out—all because I wasn't in control. I wasn't expecting it. I didn't know what to do. It triggered all of my insecurities all over again.

I was in the most picturesque place, with the most loving man, being given a beautiful marriage proposal, and all I could do was run to the bathroom and call my best friend.

I didn't say yes until 11:00 a.m. the next day.

And Nick waited. Patiently. Devotedly. With unimaginable understanding. I couldn't be loved any more.

Nick was undaunted. I was still learning.

We planned our wedding, juggling his enormous Catholic family (he has twelve siblings who produced even more offspring) with my huge Greek Orthodox family (whose count is always growing) and our mutual church family. To combine that many people with such diverse traditions was somewhat equivalent to taming a small revolution or negotiating world peace.

I desperately wanted my mom to walk me down the aisle, but I had to fight with her all the way up until a week before the wedding to convince her God would be okay with it. By tradition, my eldest brother should have. Of course, once she said yes and did it, she was never so happy and proud. She was so excited I was finally getting married. At thirty, as a Greek woman in my generation, I should have been preparing to be a grandmother.

My family thought they had lost me to the Protestant Church. Nick's family thought "pastor" was an Italian dish (pasta). And they all thought we both were crazy—calling ourselves Jesus followers and being fully devoted to God in ways they'd never seen.

But we made it. On March 30, 1996, I was walked up the aisle, praying no one would walk out when the service started because it was neither Catholic nor Orthodox. It turned out to be awesome and surreal at the same time. As I processed up the aisle, holding Mum's arm, I was taken aback by all the tears and joy. I'm not sure whether it was because our guests had only ever seen me in jeans and T-shirts or because they thought it was a miracle that Christine Caryofyllis was really getting married—in a fitted wedding dress and with professional makeup, no less.

I can still see Nick waiting for me at the end of the aisle. With each step, I marveled at our good God, who had brought him into my life, then led him to turn the car around and stop and confront me with the truth. Each step that brought me closer to Nick also reminded me how God, by healing my heart, had come close to me.

I died so that you may be free, whole, restored, healed, he whispered. He had taught me over the last year of that healing process not to settle for anything less. My past no longer defined me or my future. I was whole in order to be loved and to love in return—to reach out for others' hands just as God had reached out for mine. There was more to my calling ahead. More purpose to fulfill.

God whispered now, as he had been whispering, though I hadn't always heard it, *You are worth it*.

As I came to the head of the aisle, Nick reached out and took the hand I held out to him, open and free, whole and healed.

"I'm so glad you actually came," he whispered in my ear.

Those words have echoed in my mind for more than twenty years now. I love that I replied with a heart full of faith, absolutely undaunted and totally committed: "I wouldn't miss this for the world."

Chapter 5

HE WALKED ME THROUGH MY DISAPPOINTMENT

I sat happy and relaxed in the chair in the examining room as Dr. Kent reviewed my chart. "You're twelve weeks and six days pregnant today, Christine," he announced. "We should definitely be able to hear the baby's heartbeat. Why don't you lie on the table, and I'll go get the Doppler."

As he strode out, leaving the door open, I tried to climb onto the table. At five foot three, I'm used to stretching and reaching for things, but trying to pull myself up onto the table was a ridiculous effort. *Why do they make these tables for six-foot-tall women only?* I wondered. *Short women have babies too! Where's my pole for vaulting when I need it?*

Out of the corner of my eye, I could see a woman in the outer room trying not to laugh as she watched me make multiple approaches to conquering the climb. After several attempts, I too was tickled at how funny I must have looked. Finally, I conceded defeat and used the step stool to get up onto the table. *Someday,* I told myself, lying down, *I will be a lady. Just not today.*

Waiting for Dr. Kent's return, I thought back to one of the first times I'd been on this very table, in this very room. It seemed like just yesterday that I was pregnant with Catherine, our firstborn. *Has it really been more than two years?* Having a baby seems to blur all sense of time. *Where does it go?*

How quickly my life had changed with a child. I couldn't remember when I last slept through a whole night, finished an entire meal, or watched a television show that wasn't on Nickelodeon Junior. Of course, I wouldn't have changed a thing. I loved having a little girl, and I couldn't wait to give her a baby brother or sister. The joy that Catherine had brought into my life was about to double. I couldn't have been happier or more excited: today I would get to hear my new baby's heartbeat!

I remembered the first time I'd heard Catherine's tiny heart beating. I was shocked. It sounded out of control, like galloping horses, and I'd panicked! "What's wrong?" I'd blurted to Dr. Kent. "Why is the baby's heart racing?"

That galloping sound was perfectly normal. "Your baby is healthy," he had reassured me.

At least now I knew what to expect. Still, the sound would be like hearing a miracle all over again, a growing life inside my womb. *What a wonder God created when he allowed women to carry life. What a mystery and a privilege.* The weeks of morning sickness, the last three months of discomfort, all seemed suddenly inconsequential compared with this momentous event, the first sound to my ears of the living human being inside me.

Dr. Kent came back into the room holding a brand-new Doppler unit. "We just got this yesterday. I can't wait to try it," he said, ripping open the plastic packaging. I braced myself as he applied the cold gel on my stomach. I never liked this part. That gel was so icy and sticky. Seeing my discomfort, Dr. Kent tried to work fast. He began to move the Doppler from side to side. I waited for the soothing sound of the galloping horses. I knew from experience that it could take a few minutes for the Doppler to pick up anything, because the baby could be sleeping or lying at an awkward angle.

Dr. Kent seemed very focused. I squirmed just slightly and grew impatient. More slowly, more deliberately, he moved the instrument across my stomach.

This baby sure likes to sleep, I thought. *It must be a boy for sure, because I could hear Catherine's heart beating right away.* She was always moving, kicking, or punching me. I smiled, but Dr. Kent seemed even more focused. He continued moving the instrument, more slowly now, in wider circles across my stomach.

I remained quiet. I didn't want to miss that first beat.

Finally, he stopped and looked me in the eye. "Christine," he said, "I can't find a heartbeat."

I WAS STUNNED

No heartbeat? Before he could add anything, I blurted, "Then something must be wrong with your brand-new Doppler. Try a different one."

I couldn't read Dr. Kent's thoughts from his expression as he called his assistant to bring him the old Doppler equipment. He seemed emotionless and simply intent. Neither of us spoke as he applied more gel to my stomach and began the search again. This time the gel felt even icier as I waited for the sound of life. *Wake up, little one. C'mon. Time to wake up.*

After several quiet minutes, Dr. Kent asked me to get up. "I'm going to arrange for an ultrasound immediately," he said, all joviality gone from his voice. He picked up the phone to call the clinic. I shivered as I heard him say, "And could you make this one a priority?"

The look on his face and the tone of his voice alarmed me. This was serious.

I offered up a hasty, heartfelt prayer. *Oh, God, please, please let everything be okay with my baby. Let this just be some kind of mix-up. You gave Nick and me this child. Let the ultrasound show the baby simply sleeping or curled into an awkward position. Okay, Lord? Please?*

As I hurried out of Dr. Kent's office, I decided to walk to the clinic, just two blocks away. I needed the fresh air, and besides, I could call Nick instead of concentrating on driving and finding a parking space. I needed to hear his voice, even though I knew he would be in the middle of total mayhem at the office.

As I expected, his hello and patient listening steadied me. In a rush, I told him what was happening. "Chris," he said gently, "everything is going to be fine. You are going to have the ultrasound, and the baby will be okay. I'm so sorry I'm not there to go through this with you. Call me right away with the good report." He prayed for us just as I arrived at the clinic, and then we said goodbye.

I took a deep breath as I opened the door. With that quick walk and prayer, I felt comforted, loved, and reassured. *There's just been some mistake. This test will clear up everything,* I thought. *The ultrasound will show a perfectly healthy, growing baby in my womb.*

At the front desk, I was given a clipboard loaded with forms. I hurriedly answered all the questions, eager to get on with the test. *God,* I prayed again, *thank you for being with me.* I handed the clipboard back to the clerk.

In short order, a nurse brought me to the room set up for ultrasounds, where the technician, Jane, asked me to lie down on the table while she read over Dr. Kent's notes. When she looked up, I couldn't help but notice how deliberately she avoided making eye contact. *Don't read anything into that,* I told myself. *She is simply preoccupied with her job. Everything will be fine.*

I held still as Jane started the ultrasound. She moved the device slowly, intently, across my stomach, soon becoming fixated on one spot. As she steadied the device in that one area, she studied the computer screen intently. I tried to see what she was seeing, but nothing looked recognizable, just a gray screen with wavy lines and dots. She spent several minutes measuring, over and over, that particular spot of my stomach, highlighting it from many different angles, and never saying one word. I kept still and silent.

Finally, she stopped. "Mrs. Caine," she said, and it struck me as so formal after the friendliness of my conversation with Dr. Kent. "If you look at the lower left corner of the screen, you will see the fetus."

Fetus? The word always threw me. I never referred to Catherine as a fetus. Neither had Dr. Kent. *This is my baby,* I wanted to say, *not a thing, not something abstract. This is a new-growing person.* I tried to focus instead on what she was saying.

"Your records show that you are almost thirteen weeks pregnant, but the fetus is the size of an eight-week-old. This ultrasound indicates that the fetus stopped growing almost five weeks ago. There is no sign of a heartbeat. I am so sorry to have to tell you that it is no longer alive."

It? No longer alive?

"It is dead," she said, just like that.

Dead? I shook my head slightly in unbelief, stunned and devastated. I couldn't take my eyes off the screen. *How could this have happened?* Nick and I had prayed for this baby every day. We had spoken life to him (or her) even before we found out I was pregnant. We believed this little one was from God, given for a specific purpose and destiny. We had plans and hopes, dreams and expectations. Since we thought our baby must be a boy, we had, with excitement and love, narrowed down our choice of names to our favorites: Daniel Joseph or Jackson Elliott. *Our baby can't be dead! Wouldn't I have known? Wouldn't God want this new life he'd given us to grow and serve him? Doesn't he know how excited Nick and I were to have another baby? God wouldn't let this happen to us.*

Jane left the room as I buttoned up my shirt and collected myself to leave. Alone, I thought of all the shoulda, coulda, wouldas. *Maybe I should have planned to have children earlier. Thirty-seven is late. The older you get, the greater the risk. Perhaps I could have avoided this if I'd stopped traveling. All the time zones, the changes in food, climate, and water, the lack of rest—those things must have taken a toll on my body. What else may I have done wrong? What did I do to cause this to happen?*

The questions spun as I numbly left the clinic, full of disappointment and overcome with sadness. I had walked into Dr. Kent's office that morning full of life, hope, excitement, and dreams. I had expected to have a routine checkup, then leave and get back to the work I loved with Nick. Now I just wanted to be alone. I didn't want to talk to anyone or explain anything. I found a quiet spot outside and sat. I didn't even have the strength to cry. Never had the idea occurred to me that I might not carry this baby to full term.

For a long time, I sat alone, devastated. I prayed, *How could this have happened, God? What am I supposed to do with all the dreams Nick and I have for this child? Why did you give us this baby, just to take him away before we could even hold him, call him by name, or listen to his heartbeat and his cry and his laugh? How am I going to tell Nick? How will we tell others?*

Nick and I had made the announcement to our friends and family around the world as soon as I'd hit the eleven-week mark of confirmed pregnancy. Now I dreaded reliving the pain every time I conveyed the sad news to someone else.

We had spent an entire year thinking and praying for another child, hoping for a playmate for Catherine and figuring it might take a while for me to get pregnant because of my age. We were so surprised when it hadn't taken long at all, and the age gap between Catherine and our next baby seemed perfect. We had already adjusted our work schedules and commitments for the next year so that I could stop traveling for a while, and we had even planned out the nursery.

Catherine. How will we possibly tell our sweet little Catherine? Though just a toddler, she understood that she was going to get a baby brother or sister soon, and she was so delighted, so thrilled. We talked about it all the time. How could she possibly understand? I was heartbroken. For me. For Nick and Catherine. For everyone in our lives.

THE PAIN OF DISAPPOINTMENT

We all land in heartbreaking places at some point in life, feeling sad, alone, and perhaps drained of our courage to hope again. The reasons can be a miscarriage, like I had, or something else entirely, like when:

- your children grow up, move away, and never call
- the company to which you've devoted your years downsizes, and you get a pink slip right along with the newcomer and the slacker
- the man you love doesn't love you back, and the marriage you thought would last forever doesn't
- the child you carried and couldn't wait to hold is born with unexpected challenges
- you are diagnosed with a disease or suffer an injury for which there is no relief or cure
- it seems the one you've prayed would find Jesus never will
- colleagues betray you
- investments dwindle
- friends disappear
- dreams shatter
- best-laid plans go astray
- other Christians fail you
- people disappoint you
- you disappoint yourself

Any one of these letdowns can leave us devastated, in shock, sad, discouraged, and dismayed. Any one of these things can leave us withdrawing from life, retreating from the plans and purposes of God. And a series of disappointments can stop us from moving forward altogether, robbing everyone we might have touched with our influence had we been healed of our pain. After all, how can we help anyone else out of their disappointments if we're stuck in our own? How can we convince others of the wonder of God's promises if we are plagued with doubt ourselves?

I knew I had to resolve my own heartache and questioning, especially if I expected to keep helping others move through theirs. If I expected to keep fulfilling my calling and all that might lie ahead. If I expected to truly live an undaunted life.

But this would be a hard one to move beyond. Why is it that we can know in our heads that God has our good in mind, that he can redeem any and every circumstance, and yet still feel hugely disappointed and deeply despondent? The questions that arise in our hearts and minds are so real and, at times, gut-wrenching. We can't help but wonder.

Is God unfair? Unjust? No. He can't be, even if it looks and feels that way from our perspective. The very definitions of justice we use to determine right from wrong came from him. His Word shows us who he really is. "The LORD is righteous in all His ways and kind in all His deeds."[1]

Is he hidden? No. Though at times he can feel that way. He's promised us that he's with us at all times, that we can't get away from him. "Where can I go from your Spirit? Where can I flee from your presence?"[2]

Is he silent? Not completely. We know from experience that in seasons when it feels like God is silent, we still have his Word that is full of his messages for us, messages of love and reassurance. Still, he promises us, "Call to me and I will answer you, and will tell you great and hidden things that you have not known."[3]

If I was to move beyond the disappointment of this moment—despite all the questions that naturally arose in my heart—then I would have to remind myself of all the things about God I knew to be true, especially in the moments when they didn't feel true.

JESUS IS WITH US—ALWAYS

I understand that sometimes our experiences will be hard. Hard on our hearts. Hard to understand. Hard to endure. But I've learned they will never be impossible to move through. I understand that when we are going through a heart-wrenching season, we may feel like God is far away, even though he has promised to never leave us nor forsake us.[4] I understand that our head may tell us God is trustworthy, but in a moment of aching disappointment, our hearts can tell us he's not even there. That he doesn't see and doesn't care.

But nothing could be farther from the truth. Though we may not see him or feel him or recognize him, God is always in our midst, eager to help us heal and move forward—just like he was for the two disciples walking along the road to Emmaus a few days after Jesus' death. They felt abandoned, lost, and unsure of where to go or what to do next. They had hoped and believed that Jesus was the one sent to redeem Israel. They had believed in him, served alongside him, and followed him from town to town.

But their hopes were shattered when Jesus' body was broken, when he was beaten, bruised, crucified, and buried. Their dreams died on the cross with Jesus. Their work toward a new and better kingdom seemed over, buried with Jesus. It seemed that the past three years of spreading the gospel had all been in vain, and now they were bitterly disappointed. Having given up altogether, having lost all hope, they set out from Jerusalem.[5]

As they walked the road, they began to think and talk, trying to process their pain and make sense of all that had occurred.

"How could God let this happen?"

"What should we do now?"

Their musings sound so familiar.

Then a man met them on the road and began to walk alongside them. But they were so downcast, so crushed, they never took a good look at this fellow traveler who had joined them. Their heads, like their hearts, were bent in despair. Their focus was on themselves and their disappointment.

"What are you discussing?" the man asked.

Amazed, they stopped. "Are you the only one visiting Jerusalem who does not know the things that have happened there in these days?" one of the disciples, Cleopas, said.

"What things?" the man asked.

"About Jesus of Nazareth," the other disciple replied. "The chief priests and our rulers handed him over to be sentenced to death, and they crucified him. We had hoped that he was the one who was going to redeem Israel. And what is more, it is the third day since all this took place."

It was then that the man began explaining to them how Israel *was* going to be redeemed. He knew the promises of God by heart and explained how those promises would be fulfilled in such a way that they would change the world. A new kingdom was at hand. Walking alongside him, the disciples listened, and before they knew it, they had reached Emmaus.

When the man started to continue on, the two disciples extended an invitation. "Stay with us."

The man did, and when they all gathered at the table to eat that night, he "took bread, gave thanks, broke it and began to give it to them."[6]

Jesus! Their eyes were opened. The one walking with them through their disappointment, the one who gave them hope that God had a plan, a plan so big that even a crucifixion couldn't stop it, a plan that would use the crucifixion to redeem the world, was Jesus himself. He was not only alive but also here, right in front of them, blessing them, feeding them, walking them through their deepest discouragement, giving them a new perspective so they could move forward, undaunted. He had not left them. He had not forsaken them. And he never would.

How blind we can be! Sometimes, like the disciples, we're so focused on what's happened that we can't see Jesus walking with us through our heartache, leading us to something better ahead, giving us the courage to keep moving forward undaunted. He wants to show us that God has made a way for us that leads far beyond our disappointment. God has big plans for us—things to do, places to go, people to see. Lives to touch. Souls to direct toward him.

When we face disappointment, rather than conceding and surrendering all hope, we can pray, *Lord, I don't understand why all this has happened. But I do know you want me to keep walking, keep looking for you, keep remembering that it's what I do with disappointment that matters. Help me, as you helped those on the road to Emmaus, to surrender to you my memories of the past and my plans and dreams and hopes for the future. Help me to heal and move forward.*

Christ promises us that beyond disappointment, something better awaits us. Some mission God designed just for us, tailored, something that takes us not on a road to nowhere but to a place where we can feed others just as he has fed us, where we can bless others just as he has blessed us.

"Go," he told his disciples before he ascended into heaven. Go into all the world. Keep going past disappointment. Keep going past the disillusionment. Keep going past the despair. Keep going past pain. Keep going. Against all odds, at all times. Keep going. Go and share everything I've shared with you, and I'll be with you. "Make disciples of all nations, baptizing them in the name of the Father and of the Son and of the Holy Spirit, and teaching them to obey everything I have commanded you. And surely I am with you always, to the very end of the age."[7]

MOVING THROUGH OUR DISAPPOINTMENT

As Nick and I began to process our pain, God knew that we needed nurture and healing, refreshment and sustenance. While our natural inclination was to retreat from our friends and church family and hide, we knew that wasn't God's design. The first Sunday after Nick and I lost our baby, taking that pain and disappointment to church seemed so counterintuitive. We knew that we would be surrounded by well-intentioned church friends asking, "How's the pregnancy going? How is the baby?" and we dreaded having to answer those questions. But we knew that we needed to go to the house of God.

What I remember most about that Sunday is not how awful it was to answer people's questions about the baby and have to tell the news one more time, again and again, but rather how incredibly loving and warm our church family was to us. I had no idea how much I needed a loving community to share my burden. But God did. And as our church gathered round Nick and me in our grief, we were able to lift our eyes off our circumstances and see God's loving-kindness.

I will never forget the moment when we began to sing "Blessed Be Your Name" by Matt and Beth Redman.[8] The lyrics pierced my heart.

> Blessed be your name
> On the road marked with suffering
> Though there's pain in the offering
> Blessed be your name

I felt so empty when I began singing, but with each verse, I felt more and more emotion, and soon the tears came. The cry of the psalmist broke something in me and then filled my empty soul. The weight of my grief and the burden of feeling alone spilled out, and peace and confidence in the Lord's love and care poured in. The words became my sacrifice, an offering to the Lord, who had already walked the road of suffering before me and now returned to meet me on it. I was in communion with him, knowing he wanted to bless me with "beauty instead of ashes, the oil of joy instead of mourning, and a garment of praise instead of a spirit of despair."[9] A spiritual exchange took place: I magnified the Lord instead of my disappointment. I began to remember his mercies more than my hurt. I began to tap into his joy inside me. I began to pull on the strength his joy gives. "Though the fig tree does not bud, and there are no grapes on the vines, though the olive crop fails and the fields produce no food, though there are no sheep in the pen and no cattle in the stalls, yet I will rejoice in the LORD, I will be joyful in God my Savior."[10]

Because I had lost something precious, everything around me seemed dead, yet God remained good. Like Habakkuk, in that I was able to rejoice.

THE APPOINTMENTS IN OUR DISAPPOINTMENTS

For each of us, there is so much more waiting beyond our disappointments, just like it was for the disciples on the road to Emmaus. There are appointments God has set up for us to keep. People for us to encounter. Good works for each of us to do. I can't help but find it interesting that the word *appointment* comes from within the word *disappointment*.

I've often marveled at that because I've seen again and again how disappointments take something from us—a dream, a piece of our heart, maybe whole chunks of it. But disappointments leave something too—a gift, an opportunity, a chance to create change, to move from the valley of the shadow of death to new horizons, to fulfill a calling we never anticipated, and to bring others with us on that road.

The enemy would like us to feel such a depth of disappointment that we never find our way back to the plan we know God has for us or discover the one we may never have considered. If the enemy can only convince us to stay stuck in our disappointment, then he knows we'll miss many of our God appointments. I understand there are some disappointments that seem so big, so inconceivable, that we can't imagine ever being able to move beyond them. Nick and I have walked with friends through unbearable losses. We've grieved and cried with them and gently helped them move forward again. We've encouraged them as they have found new futures they never could have imagined before.

Like so many others, I discovered that because of the kind of pain I'd endured in losing a baby, I could help others through their pain. I now had a firsthand perspective and I could allow God to use that to help other women in a more specific way.

Before my baby died, I had for years spoken at women's conferences and met women who'd lost a child before birth. I had learned that one in four women experience a miscarriage, but before my loss, that was just a number, a cold statistic. Afterward I understood what those women were feeling. Out of my own heartache and disappointment grew an even deeper sense of compassion for mothers who lose their unborn children. The pain is real yet often unacknowledged, because it's invisible, because the mother never had a chance to hold the baby in her arms, to feel its heart beating next to hers. Now I too had experienced this invisible loss, and the heartache had been harsh and unforgettable. I would never again look at such invisible yet profound pain the same way. I would not be dismissive of the hurt someone else felt or expressed. I wanted to make sure that other bereaved mothers received time, attention, and spiritual and emotional medicine, whether they'd had to let go of their child before it was born or even years after.

THE BIRTH OF MY DREAM

Almost two years after losing my baby, I discovered I was pregnant again. I should have been elated, and I was extremely happy, of course, but after what I had been through, I had to constantly fight to stay in a place of faith and joy. If you've had a miscarriage, then you understand the tug-of-war between excitement and apprehension. One moment you're on top of the world, full of hope, thanking God for this new life, and then the next you're fighting a wave of fear because you're remembering what could happen, what did happen.

On top of my own concerns were those of the doctors. They had treated me as high-risk during my last pregnancy because I was thirty-seven—older than most obstetricians like a mom to be— and now that I was thirty-nine, they were treating me even more carefully. Especially after having suffered a miscarriage.

They wanted me to know the risks, understand the medical possibilities, and be prepared for potential outcomes. They meant well. They were performing their duties responsibly, but when they wanted me to read pamphlets on all the risks associated with being thirty-nine and pregnant, I considered it and then chose not to read them. It was a personal decision but one I felt I had to make to keep my heart and mind in a place of faith and not fear. I wasn't in denial. Not at all. I knew the risks without reading the pamphlets, but I had prayed and believed for this child, and I had to put my trust in God. To do that, I didn't need to read bad news; I needed to keep my focus on God's promises. Especially before every doctor appointment to check on the baby's growth.

I was so glad Nick and I were in this fight of faith together. Like any parents, we wrestled over when to tell Catherine. We didn't want her heart to be disappointed again. We debated on when to tell our friends, knowing they would stand with us in faith but not wanting to put them through any emotional ups and downs. We knew they deserved to know because they were so loyal and faithful. After much thought and conversation, we chose to wait until I was sixteen weeks along to break the news.

In all those moments, it was hard to know what to be sure of, but we knew to put our trust in God. We knew to keep doing what we were called to do. We kept traveling and speaking and seeing souls won to Christ, with all the faith we had.

The fearful thoughts still came, because the enemy will always be persistent. And anytime I had a twinge of pain, I had to control my thinking and speak and pray the Scriptures we were standing on. I had to cast down thoughts one at a time, taking every thought captive minute by minute, hour by hour, day by day.[11] I had to confess faith one word at a time, holding on to what I believed, trusting that he who promised is always faithful.[12] I had to pray one prayer at a time, trusting that he was listening, that he was near, that he would strengthen me.[13]

I had to live undaunted, despite what I was facing. But that didn't mean I was unchallenged, unaware, uninformed, or uncertain. Undaunted faith didn't mean I was denying the reality of fear or my circumstances. But it did mean I was determined to keep moving forward one step at a time despite the anxiety and fear that kept knocking at my heart's door.

I fought the good fight of faith one step, prayer, thought, day, opportunity, experience, challenge, and doctor appointment at a time. I knew I couldn't control the outcome of the process, but I also knew the God who would carry me through it and protect me in it. I knew I couldn't let the past dictate my present or my future. I chose to let God use where I was—the process I was in—to strengthen me even more for the future that lay ahead. I had to trust that his grace would be sufficient, that the same God who had brought me this far would take me the rest of the way.

And he did.

I can't describe the joy I felt when Sophia Joyce Grace was born. She was perfect in every way. Beautiful. Everything we'd dreamed. And yet I was well aware that having a healthy baby is not how everyone's pregnancy story unfolds.

I will never get to hold my second child this side of eternity, and you may never get to hold one of yours, or all of yours. Your heartbreaking disappointment may be something else entirely. Whatever it is, God knows. He sees. He cares. He's been walking alongside you. Ever since you felt that loss. He's never left you nor forsaken you. And now he's ready to show you the way forward to the future you might never have considered. To use you in ways you might never have imagined. Lean into him. Trust him. And dare to do all he has called you to do.

PART 3

GOD KNOWS MY FEAR

Chapter 6

I OVERCAME MY BIGGEST FEAR

⸻⸺∞⸺⸻

Ladies and gentlemen, there is no need to panic."

Panic? Why would any captain of any flight say there's no need to panic unless there is a need to panic? Nick and I had barely made ourselves comfortable on a flight from Chicago to Raleigh, North Carolina, when the captain said the P word. And I'd been doing just fine until he made that announcement. Definitely not what I wanted to hear at thirty thousand feet.

We'd been airborne only twenty minutes, and nothing had seemed out of the ordinary. Even so, the mere mention of the word *panic* changed everything. My heart started to race. Passengers all around gasped, and then there was an eerie silence as we waited for the captain to tell us more.

"We are having trouble getting the landing gear up," he continued. "Rather than continue on to Raleigh, we'll have to turn around and try to land in Chicago."

Try? That's another word you never want to hear in midair.

I gulped as I watched fear touch everyone up and down the aisle. Some passengers bowed their heads and began to audibly pray.

Others started to cry. Flight attendant call buttons lit up the overhead panels like a Christmas tree as people begged for more information.

I overheard one lady ask her husband, "Are we going to crash and die?"

A few years earlier, I would have been one of the panicked ones. I probably would have been the most distraught person onboard. But now, even though my heart was definitely beating faster and I could feel myself shift to a state of heightened awareness, I wasn't clutching the armrests or bracing myself against the seat, losing all reason and confidence. Instead I slipped my hand into Nick's, grateful for his ever-calm demeanor.

True to form, he began quietly praying for us—not in fear but as if he were asking a blessing on the morning meal or thanking God for the beautiful day. He committed the pilot, the passengers, and a safe landing to the Lord. Then he leaned into me and whispered in my ear, "We'll be fine, Chris. God has not brought us this far for it all to end like this. He is with us and has our backs. You don't need to be afraid of anything." With that, he squeezed my hand, reclined his seat, and closed his eyes. Within a few minutes, believe it or not, he gave every impression of having drifted off to sleep.

While I couldn't replicate Nick's complete calm, I relished it. Something powerful is transferred from one person to another when fear is not allowed to rule their heart. I couldn't help but marvel at his lying there, eyes closed, not a worry in the world. *So typically Nick*, I thought. *While everyone else panics, he just sits back with rock-solid confidence in the goodness and protection of God.* Nick has been this way for as long as I've known him, able to live out Paul's instruction to the Philippians: "Be anxious for nothing, but in everything by prayer and supplication, with thanksgiving, let your requests be made known to God; and the peace of God, which surpasses all understanding, will guard your hearts and minds through Christ Jesus."[1] I was grateful for Nick's quiet strength and confidence and thanked God for it, wanting more of that same quality myself.

By nature, I'm the opposite. I continually have to remind myself that just because everyone else is freaking out doesn't mean I have to. Left to my own devices, if I'd been writing to the Philippians, I probably would have begun, "Be anxious for everything, because you never know what might happen. You know, just in case something does happen."

No doubt, I struggle to simply cast my cares on the Lord, like 1 Peter 5:7 says. There is nothing simple about complete, unquestioning trust, and I've wrestled with God over this much of my life. Even now, after decades of seeing how God never leaves us nor forsakes us and always works all things together for good, I still catch myself having to choose to trust, having to remind myself that he is with me always, even in situations like this one in which the danger is real and undeniable.[2]

But now, in that hushed and tense plane, I wasn't wrestling. We—like all the other passengers who had no choice—could do nothing but wait, hope, and pray that we would land safely in Chicago. I was on high alert but not panicked, watchful but not wilting. I sat calmly next to Nick, still reclined peacefully. I looked out the window onto a beautiful, clear night sky, lit by stars and tiny lights on the plane's wings, and prayed, because I had faith, not fear. I couldn't help but smile.

God, I thought thankfully, *how things have changed.*

FEAR LIMITS US

My remaining calm on that flight was nothing less than miraculous, because years ago flying was one of my greatest fears. Yes, me. The one whom God has called to run laps around the globe. I used to be one of those people who got on a plane only if there was no other option. If I could get somewhere by car, bus, train, bicycle, scooter, or on foot, then I did—whatever it took to avoid boarding a big mass of metal expected to, beyond all logic, somehow stay up in the sky. I can't count the times when a bit of turbulence on a flight sent my mind imagining every worst-case scenario, such as the engines stopping in midair and the plane falling off the radar somewhere over the ocean or bursting into flames over a city. The possibilities terrified me.

And because my work required me to travel from one continent to another over and over again in any given year, my fear was definitely a problem. I'd prayed for God to take me wherever people needed to hear the good news of grace, and he had honored that prayer. He opened doors across the country and around the world for me to speak. To lead people to Christ. To teach his Word. Since my twenties, I have known that this is what he has called me to do. But because I lived in Australia—the land *far* down under—the first twenty years of my ministry life, going almost anywhere in the world meant flying, plain and simple.

Only it wasn't so simple for me. I'd said yes to God, but if I was to make good on that commitment, then God would have to do a work in me. I would have to let him lead me out of my fear and into a place of overcoming faith. Somehow. Some way. As hard as it seemed, I couldn't let fear stop me from fulfilling his call on my life.

But in the meantime, flying taxed my mind, body, and spirit. Every. Single. Flight. I would sit bolt upright, my hands wrapped around the armrests, gripping them the entire journey. Out of Australia, most of my flights not only were extraordinarily long— because they stretched across an ocean whether I was traveling east or west—but also felt endless and exhausting. They fatigued me. I would arrive at my destination anxious and arrested by fear— hardly the state people hoped for in a guest speaker.

The terror and anxiety I experienced would begin a week before I was scheduled to leave. I would break out in a sweat every time I even thought about getting on the plane. My heart would race and my chest would tighten. I had to force myself to think about other things, just like Philippians teaches us to do: "Whatsoever things are true, whatsoever things are honest, whatsoever things are just, whatsoever things are pure, whatsoever things are lovely, whatsoever things are of good report; if there be any virtue, and if there be any praise, think on these things. Those things, which ye have both learned, and received, and heard, and seen in me, do: and the God of peace shall be with you."[3]

I needed God's peace more than anything. You'd think that once I landed, I would be relieved, but my condition wasn't any better. As I exited the plane and entered the airport terminal, my legs would be like jelly, and often I would feel disoriented. I remember once trying to hold a conversation with the person who picked me up at the airport. I was still so shaken by flying that I could barely utter a coherent sentence. I'm sure they presumed that I was suffering from jet lag, but the time zone differences were the least of the reasons for my exhaustion.

I remember the day I knew enough was enough, and my solution must have been quite humorous to God. I was returning from a trip, so drained by the emotional and physical energy required to fight my fears that I decided I was through with this. I told God that although I wanted to go and help people, I could no longer face the pressure or endure the process of getting on an airplane. I would limit myself to going to places I could drive to. *I'm willing to go, Lord, as long as the transportation is on the ground, within my comfort zone. I'll go anywhere for you, as long as I don't have to fly.*

As long as.

Can you imagine? That was how I was talking to God, the God who left everything in heaven to come to us, the God who asks us to go and do likewise. *I will,* I said. *I can. I'm going—as long as.*

I'm sure he had a good laugh that day! Especially since he knows the end of our lives from the beginning.[4]

FEAR HAS A MISSION

We all fear something until we learn to overcome it. Muggers lurking in dark alleyways. Losing our wallet. Losing our job and being left penniless. Dying or being injured in an automobile or airplane crash. Being bitten by a wild animal. Getting stung by a poisonous insect. Enduring the ridicule of hecklers when we speak publicly. Facing rejection or disinterest upon meeting new people. Losing a child. Being abandoned by a loved one.

Some of us fear failing. Others fear success. "What if I stick my neck out and fail?" we say. "What if the business gets too big too fast and I can't keep up, or my customers see how little I really know and what an amateur I am?"

How can we live undaunted if we are paralyzed by fear?

We can't.

To live undaunted is to show courage and resolution. It's to live unafraid, undismayed, unflinching, unshrinking, unabashed— fearless. It's being bold, brave, gritty, audacious, daring, and confident, even when we face opportunities not to be.

But it's a fight, I know.

Some fears are rational, such as the healthy fear of walking a tightrope above a canyon, an activity in which the chances of injury or death are unacceptably high. Other fears are not so rational, like another one of mine—being in too small or tight a space or being confined. It does me no good to reassure myself rationally that just because the space is small, it doesn't mean the walls will collapse around me and suffocate me. Some fears are subtle, like a general apprehension or worry, while others are dramatic, like dread and terror.

When we're young, we may fear imaginary beasts in the dark, under our bed or in the closet. When we're older, the invisible but oh-so-real monsters of disease and death may be what we fear is lurking in the dark. We may even live consumed with anxiety that all our secrets will be brought to light.

Whatever our story, whether our fear is subdued or strong, rational or irrational, the danger real or imagined, fear has a mission: It will always try to stop us, trip us up, and put our lives on hold. It will always seek to immobilize us and divert our attention away from daring to fulfill God's call on our lives.

GOD HAS A STRATEGY

I don't know where all my fears came from, but I know that many of the ones I've overcome are the result of the abuse I suffered as a child. So many of our fears can be traced back to our experiences and what we believe about ourselves because of those events. I saw this so clearly when I became a mother and realized how fear could so quickly and irrationally rise up in my girls.

I remember one day when we were traveling on a lengthy road trip, and a storm came upon us like a monster out of nowhere. Catherine was five, and she had begun our journey home by falling asleep with sunlight streaming through the car windows. After sleeping for a couple of hours, she woke to see the weather's fury unleashed outside.

Gray skies had darkened and a hard rain had turned into a hailstorm just as we pulled into our driveway. Nick grabbed our bags as I grabbed the girls, hurrying everything and everyone inside. We'd barely made it indoors when the storm reached new and frightening heights. Behind us, hail pummeled the car, denting the hood and roof, even cracking the windows. Racing to the front windows of our home, we could see windows of cars and houses up and down the street breaking. Roof tiles were shattering and falling to the ground. Water was splashing violently out of everyone's backyard pools and over the fences. Thunder punctuated the incessant pounding of the hail. We heard a tree, struck by lightning and gale-force winds, splinter and fall through the roof of the house behind us. Another fell across our neighbor's driveway.

Sophia, then just a baby, slept through it all, still snugged in her car seat. But Catherine was terrified, and she began to scream and cry. Even after the hail stopped, she could not be comforted. She cried and shrieked until finally, exhausted, she fell into a fitful sleep.

I expected that she would wake at peace, and the fear would have passed like the hail outside. That she would forget about it all. I was wrong.

She rose the next morning asking if it was going to rain and hail again. She worriedly looked out the window all day, trying to gauge the weather. For days following, she would ask Nick and me, sometimes as many as five times in a morning or afternoon, if it was going to rain. Every time we needed to take the car anywhere, she obsessed over the weather. If it started to rain while we were in the car, she would cry. If we were home when the rain began, she would run into her room and pull the curtains. She would not play outside with her friends if there was even a hint of gray sky.

Catherine's fear of storms was so strong that she grew willing to change everything else in her life to avoid them. That's when I knew I had to intervene. She couldn't live her life in fear of rain, because one thing we can be sure of about the future is that rain will come. There will be storms—of every kind—and hiding from them won't stop them. The only way Catherine could shut herself away from the storms was by shutting herself away from life.

The irony of her behavior was not lost on me. I had spent much of my life shutting myself off from fully experiencing life because of my fear of flying. But avoiding my fear had not immunized me from danger, because danger comes no matter how much we try to keep it at bay. On flights. During road trips. On any given day. Trying to live a safe, controlled life won't stop danger or the fear that can accompany it. The only thing we can do is face fear head-on and learn to defeat it. If we don't, it will take root in our hearts and take over our lives. Just like it had done to me. Just like it was trying to do to Catherine.

Jesus understands this. He knows what the enemy will always throw at us. How the enemy will use fear to control us. That's why, during a powerful storm on the Sea of Galilee, he used a situation involving Peter, one of his closest disciples, to teach us all the power of fear and an even more powerful strategy to overcome it.[5]

Peter had been a fisherman by trade. He was used to choppy waters and restless seas. He was used to dangerous conditions, and he knew how to navigate storms. He practically lived on the water.

But like all of us, he wasn't immune to the fear that can come with any storm.

After he and the disciples ended a day of ministry with Jesus, feeding thousands of people, they sailed out onto the sea while Jesus went up a mountainside to pray. Late in the night, waves began to buffet the boat as the wind grew stronger and stronger. And rather than dissipate quickly, the storm intensified, lasting well into the predawn hours. Knowing this story that appears in three of the four gospels, I can imagine what Peter was experiencing: his fears were whispering in his head, just as they were in the minds of the other disciples on the boat.

The winds are too fierce. The waves are too high. The boat is too fragile for these gales.

As the story goes, everyone in the boat began to cower in fear, their focus fixed on all the dangers of the storm. Then, just as Peter was about to give up, he looked out on the water and saw . . . Jesus?

Yes, Jesus. Walking on the water. Walking through the storm. Making his way to them. He called out to Peter to step out into the storm as well, to step out of the boat and onto the water, to step into the danger. What Jesus didn't invite Peter to do was to step out into fear. No, he was inviting him to take a step of faith.

And Peter wanted to do it. His heart was pulling him in the right direction.

"Come," Jesus said to him.[6]

Believing that with Jesus he could do anything, Peter took that step of faith, his eyes fixed on the Lord. One step out of the boat, and just like that, he was walking through the storm, right on top of the water, undaunted, defying the danger, doing the miraculous.

But then an especially large gust of wind swept over Peter, spray whipped his face, and his attention was diverted from Jesus and back to the storm. His fears began whispering again.

The waves are too high. The wind is too fierce. Jesus is too far away.

But Jesus wasn't too far away. He's never too far away. Peter just quit looking at him. He took his focus off Jesus and looked back at the storm raging around him. His vision became clouded, his sight deceived. And the consequences were instant.

Sinking in the water, Peter cried out to Jesus, "Lord, save me!"[7]

"Immediately," the Bible says, "Jesus reached out his hand and caught him. 'You of little faith,' he said, 'why did you doubt?'"[8]

Why do *we* doubt?

Jesus beckons us to come. If we stay focused on him, we will be able to go anywhere and do whatever is required of us. If we take our eyes off him and stare at the storm, at the danger, then we will surely sink. We will never reach the lost. We will never go to the millions trapped in the darkness of human trafficking. We will never help the millions without clean water, or the multitudes suffering abuse, disease, famine, injustice, loneliness, and sheer hopelessness.

To get to them, we will most likely have to walk on water.

This is what God was showing me as I sought him on how to help Catherine. I knew that my daughter feared storms so much that she was willing to forsake many things she loved, like fun and friends. If she didn't conquer her fear of a little rain, then she would be overwhelmed by even lesser storms as she—and her fear—grew. If I didn't help her, she could one day be paralyzed by fear, like I had been—like Peter had been.

So the next rainy day that came, I scooped up Catherine in my arms and took her outside. At first she cried, but I insisted on making a game of the rain. I began to jump and stomp in the puddles. I laughed at the sky. I rejoiced in the rain. I showed her how fun it was to be drenched in the refreshing downpour. Surprised by my thrill and my absence of fear, Catherine stopped crying and started laughing along with me. Soon she let me lower her onto the ground, where she began stomping in the puddles too.

Now I can't keep Catherine inside when it rains. She grabs her sister, and they put on their gumboots to run into the puddles and splash. The very thing she once feared has become her playground.

The transformation I saw in Catherine shows us how fear and faith cannot coexist. She left one to step into the other, just like I had done. Yes, it was a process. Yes, it was a choice. But I watched her face as she transitioned from one to the other. It was amazing to see the shift in her perspective and see peace fill her heart. I watched her choose to believe me instead of her fear.

Like Catherine, when I faced my own fears, I had to choose whether I was going to believe God's truth or the lies of the enemy. Was I going to yield to my emotions or focus my attention on God and his Word? Was I going to choose fear of the world or faith in the one who has overcome the world?

I chose to trust the Creator of the universe, the one who hung the moon and placed the stars and fixed the sky. Won't you join me?

"Go," he says to us all, "and make disciples of all nations, baptizing them in the name of the Father and of the Son and of the Holy Spirit, and teaching them to obey everything I have commanded you."[9]

And he faithfully gives us the promise that makes it all possible, that makes it possible for us to live undaunted: "Surely I am with you always, to the very end of the age."[10]

He doesn't ask us to go as long as or if or after he removes all danger and takes away all fear. No, he asks us to go in spite of and even if and anyway. He says simply, *Believe. Go with me.*

He's been saying this all my life, giving me the courage to look fear in the face and dare to go where he is calling me to go.

When I wanted to go to Bible college but feared I'd get booted out once the professors discovered how little I really knew, Jesus asked, *Will you go with me?*

"Yes, Lord," I told him. "I'll go anyway, because I want to better know and understand your Word and pass on the good news."

When I was afraid to marry because my trust had been broken and I was suffering from hidden wounds, he asked, *But Chris, will you go with me?*

"Yes, Lord," I said. "I'll go, even though I'm afraid of being hurt again, because I don't want to miss out on the relationships you ordained for me or the love that's waiting for me."

When God began to open doors for me to talk to teenagers in

high school, I was terrified. "What if they ridicule and heckle me or simply refuse to listen?"

But Jesus asked, *Will you go with me?*

"Yes, Lord. I'll go even though they might not listen to me, because what if just one life is touched and transformed? It will be worth it for that one."

And when he brought me opportunities to share about him around the world, and to get there not on a slow boat but on one of the jet planes that terrified me, he asked once more, *Will you go with me?*

When I was arrested by posters of missing children in the Thessaloniki airport, I heard him again: *Will you go with me?* I had no idea how, when, or where, but I said yes anyway, and A21 was birthed.

In everything he's asked me to do, I knew that I had a choice. Jesus always gives us a choice. I could choose to allow my fears to rule me, or I could believe that the God who made the heavens and called me was unstoppable and unafraid of the gravity he created. If he wanted me to cross the globe to be his hands and feet in getting to one of the lost and lonely, the hungry and thirsty, the trafficked and abused, then he could uphold a plane in the sky.

GOD GAVE US LIFE

What do you fear? What part of living are you avoiding because of fear? When we allow fear to dictate how we spend our days, we will allow life to pass us by. We will miss out on the best that God has planned for us. The list of things we can fear is endless.

- Heights
- Crowds
- Sharing our thoughts or speaking aloud
- Being made fun of or being left out
- Taking a risk and failing
- Rejection
- Being alone

When we let fear run our lives, we close ourselves off from anything that might hurt us or cost us or make us uncomfortable, including opportunities to serve God and walk in his promises. God calls us to serve with what we have and with who we are, but if we don't lean into him and overcome our fears, then we won't fulfill what he's called us to do. We won't touch the people we're destined to influence.

- The coworker you were meant to mentor
- The single woman who would love someone to sit with her in church
- The new family in the neighborhood who could use an introduction to the community
- The young women in recovery who could use an encouraging role model like you, someone who knows how to write a resume and dress for an interview
- The lives that could benefit from the initiative God has called you to launch
- The families whose livelihood could be provided by the business you are called to start

Jesus warned us, "The thief comes only to steal and kill and destroy."[11] Fear is a thief like that. It can cause us to hold back and run away from the very assignments God has designed just for us. But if we'll trust, if we'll lean into Jesus, if we'll keep our eyes on him, we can rest in what he promised: "I have come that they may have life, and have it to the full."[12]

To. The. Full.

GOD DELIVERS US

Jesus knew we would be afraid. He knew that we would doubt. That's why he tells us again and again in the Bible, "Fear not." Hundreds of times he tells us not to fear. In so many stories in Scripture, when God sent angels to people, the first words they spoke were, "Fear not."[13]

It's as though God were like a mother who reaches for her child crying in the storm, wraps her arms around her trembling heart, and says soothingly over and over, "It's okay. I'm here with you. Don't be afraid."

Isn't that what I did for Catherine?

Isn't that what Jesus did for me?

For years, I yearned for deliverance from my fears. I prayed fervently for God to remove my fears, especially my fear of flying. Out of desperation, I often demanded, "Why won't you just take this fear from me? After all, I'm getting on this plane for you!"

But instead of instantaneously delivering me, instead of giving in to my anxious demands, in his tender mercy he guided me back to his Word: "God has not given us a spirit of fear, but of power and of love and of a sound mind."[14]

Fear is not from God, and it's not more powerful than him. He's given me all I need to fight fear, to overcome it and its effects, by giving me his power. By leading me to receive and believe his love for me. By revealing to me that I have a sound mind because I have the mind of Christ.[15] Because I have been saved, because his Spirit lives in me, I have the capacity to live free from fear.

What I had to do was develop that capacity. I had to tap into the power, love, and sound mind God had given me. When I leaned into his power, he enabled me to move forward in courage. That didn't mean I ignored fear's presence or denied its threats. No, not at all. Courage, after all, is not the absence of fear; it's the will to persevere even in the face of fear. To move forward believing God more than the fear that wants us to buckle at the knees. To trust God and keep going even if we still feel afraid. How many times have we clung to a promise from God's Word, only to let go of it in the face of fear? Leaning into God's power enables us to hold on to the promise, to not let the spirit of fear get bigger than the promise in our hearts and minds.

He's given us all three—power, love, and a sound mind—to help us overcome our fear. Jesus knows the power of love to strengthen our faith, to keep our focus on him and not on the fear taunting us. When he had risen from the dead, he appeared to the disciples, and addressing Peter specifically, he questioned him about love. "Do you love me?" he asked Peter.[16] It's really a question for every one of us. Do we believe his unconditional love for us? Do we trust him? Do we trust him more than we lean into our fears?

To love Jesus is to keep our eyes on him. Isn't that what Jesus wanted Peter to do when he bade him to come on the water? "Look at me, Peter. Keep your eyes on me." I believe so.

When we keep our eyes on Jesus, he releases us from the constraints that bind us in fear. We are no longer restricted and trapped. We are free. Our world and our lives enlarge, and the possibilities for the miraculous increase. We achieve the impossible by focusing on the God with whom all things are possible. We reach and rescue the people who have fallen through society's cracks. We rescue slaves who otherwise would be captive still. We help the defeated who otherwise would languish. We find the lost. We bring healing to the damaged and diseased. We open the eyes of the blind.

By staying mentally and emotionally focused on him, by holding on to the sound mind he has given us, by renewing it according to the Word daily,[17] we mentally and emotionally go places we never imagined, without sinking or being swallowed by our fears.

I can't count the times I've reached for the Word and prayed Philippians to keep renewing my mind according to the truth, to hold on to peace again and again. "Be anxious for nothing, but in everything by prayer and supplication, with thanksgiving, let your requests be made known to God; and the peace of God, which surpasses all understanding, will guard your hearts and minds through Christ Jesus."[18]

I can't count the times I've reached for verses like the following to steady my heart and remind myself of the truth.

- "The LORD is my light and my salvation—whom shall I fear? The LORD is the stronghold of my life—of whom shall I be afraid?"[19]
- "Fear not, for I am with you; be not dismayed, for I am your God. I will strengthen you, yes, I will help you, I will uphold you with My righteous right hand."[20]

To walk in faith and not give fear control, I have to lean into and believe God and his Word. Continually. That's how God did a work in me and delivered me from all my fears.

I CAN FLY

As the captain navigated our plane back toward Chicago, the power of Jesus' presence that comes from keeping my eyes on him is what kept me calm on that flight. With malfunctioning landing gear, we were in real danger of crashing upon landing. As the captain announced our approach to O'Hare Airport and instructed us in how to prepare, I watched the people around me brace themselves for the worst. They held on to the armrests of their seats or the hand or arm of the person sitting next to them. Many audibly prayed.

I closed my eyes.

My hand in Nick's, I prayed silently, *Lord, I am ever so grateful you did not let me succumb to my fear of flying but rather helped me choose to push through that fear. There were times I never thought I would or could get back on a plane, but I so wanted your will and purpose for my life. How many times have I had to choose to get on a flight afraid, and yet every time, you have been with me, comforting me, enabling me, strengthening me. And because of that, I have been able to go to so many cities and nations around the world and reach people I never would have been able to reach otherwise.*

And thinking of God's promise in 2 Timothy 1:7, I stood on God's truth: *Lord, like every other time, I choose to remind myself that you have given me a spirit not of fear but of power and of love and of a* *sound mind.*

I was never so thankful, so affirmed in my faith, as when I heard and felt rubber hitting the tarmac. All of the passengers erupted in applause. As we decelerated down the long runway, we passed awaiting ground personnel, police cars, fire trucks, and ambulances—all with sirens blasting.

Yet we landed without incident, and within minutes the door of the plane was opened, letting light stream in as if it were a brand-new day. And I went on to speak where God had sent me.

I once feared flying with a paralyzing fear that kept me bound to the island of Australia. But because Jesus calmed my fears, just like he did Peter's, just like I did Catherine's, the very thing I once feared became my vehicle to minister to more people in more places.

I know we'll never escape living in a dark world. Rain will fall. Storms will come. Lightning will strike. And as long as we live, there always will be something to lose, even little pieces of ourselves. The people we love, the lives we cherish—there is always something at risk, something dear. Something to cause fear.

But Jesus didn't give us a spirit of fear. He gave us power, love, and a sound mind to overcome the work of the enemy. He gave us peace and joy. And he's invited us to come.

Step out of the boat. Keep your eyes on Jesus. And dare to do all he's called you to do.

Chapter 7

I REMEMBERED WHAT IT WAS TO BE LOST

That day in Thessaloniki when Sonia turned to me and asked, "Why didn't you come sooner?" her demand was visceral, desperate, and honest. She had lived through a horror most of us can only try to understand. She had been denied food, water, even air. She had watched her friends die and had been forced to remain locked up with their bodies. She had been attacked, degraded, and enslaved, terrified into submission.

How could she not question me? How could she not question the integrity of my God? And how could I not answer her with the rawest honesty possible? The pain she had known was unfathomable.

You and I may not be among the modern-day slaves on this earth who will ever suffer as Sonia did—desperate to be found, to be rescued, to be restored—but we are believers, which means we have known what it is to be lost.

Lost is what we once were. Before Jesus found us. Before Jesus adopted us. Before he began to grow us up into him. And lost is what we once felt. Before Jesus healed our hearts. Before Jesus helped us find our way. Before he set us on the path to discovering our calling. Lost is a feeling we have all shared, a feeling God wants us to always remember. I'll never forget the day God reminded me of what he wants us never to forget.

A TRIP TO THE DAINTREE

Our Jeep, driven by Mick and now sliding out of control, lurched and fishtailed down the steep, muddy road. The curve up ahead was approaching much too fast, and the brakes were futile in all the mud. Watching the steep mountainside flying by, I gritted my teeth and closed my eyes, as I knew we were about to go off the side of the road. I braced for whatever would happen.

Mick kept pumping the brakes and cut the wheel, first one direction and then another. He tried every technique to stay on the road, but it was no use. Hanging on for our very lives, we were helpless as the Jeep nosedived straight down the mountain. As it crashed through all the underbrush, we bounced into each other and off the Jeep's roof and sides. At the mercy of gravity and physics, we slid faster and faster, until we reached the bottom and slammed into a huge, muddy ditch.

There were five of us—Kylie, Sally, Mick, Paul, and me—all good friends, all still single. We were on the last day of a summer trip and had decided to drive through the Daintree Rainforest, one of Australia's natural wonders and among the oldest preserved ecosystems in the world. Using a faded map we found discarded at a diner, we'd chosen what looked like an interesting route and set out. We'd had a wonderful and scenic drive up to this point—eucalyptus and red gum trees so large that our group of five could not even clasp our hands together and encircle one vine-covered trunk. Miles of orchids, ferns, and wild ginger stretched beneath palms whose giant green branches brushed us like fans as we walked past. Cascading waterfalls with misty sprays cooled us in the tropical heat.

It had been great fun with amazing views. Until now. Until we found ourselves in a bog.

"I couldn't stop!" Mick gasped. "Everybody okay?"

Stunned and shaken, and ever so slowly, we each checked ourselves for broken bones or gashes. One by one, we all responded with great relief that we were okay.

I pried my fingers off the seat back in front of me, which I'd grabbed onto for dear life. *Oh well,* I decided, rubbing my neck, *there's nothing more to say or do but get out of the Jeep and start pushing it out of the mud.*

Remembering the slurp and ooze that surrounded my legs when I had stepped into the swale earlier that day, I thought of all the mud outside the Jeep. *Yuck. I wonder what else is in here.* I was still up for an adventure, but none of this was what any of us had ever expected.

JUST A WALK IN THE WOODS

For the next two hours, we all five pushed, shoved, lifted, and waded in the mud, trying to dislodge our tiny, Tonka-like vehicle. Finally, it budged, and we moved it to reasonably level and dry ground. As we surveyed the area, it looked as if, with our four-wheel drive, we'd be able to make it back to the road. Tired and covered in brown slime, we rested a minute against the Jeep's side before attempting our plan.

When Mick jumped into the driver's seat to start the engine, he turned the key, and after a momentary sputter, there was nothing. He turned the key again. Sputter, sputter. Nothing. At first, we thought maybe mud had clogged the fuel line. Then Paul pointed to the gas gauge flashing red. We'd been having so much fun that none of us noticed that we'd used up the gas in the main tank and had been running on the reserve. The slide must have burned the last of our fuel.

"Well," I said, laughing, "looks like we're walkin'."

"Yeah," Kylie said. "But surely, given the amount of time we've driven, we can't be that far from the end of the road."

"There ought to be someplace ahead where we can call for help," Mick said.

Though none of us had a cell phone, our spirits were high.

"This is going to make one great story," I said, eyebrows raised, grinning.

We started down the road, laughing and playing, not particularly worried. After all, we'd just survived what could have been a fatal crash.

Before long, though, we started to grow anxious to reach somewhere that looked more like civilization. We seemed to be going deeper into the rainforest rather than coming out. I began to realize how thirsty I was and, come to think of it, hungry too. My feet were hurting because flip-flops weren't the best footwear for walking through a dense rainforest. The sunlight, already dim under the canopy of trees, was beginning to fade. Cool breezes filtered through the wet foliage from the coast, and after being so hot earlier, I now felt chilled in my thin T-shirt and shorts.

We walked on, still merry, but our laughter was subdued a notch as we each entertained the same wish: A shower. Something to eat. Something to drink. Silently, I prayed we'd find our way out of the woods sooner rather than later. I wasn't scared. I just wanted to get back to the fun of our wooded wonderland adventure. I felt sure we weren't far from a place to grab dinner, or at least a snack, fuel for the Jeep, and maybe even a lift back to it so we could be on our way. I figured no one would put a road to nowhere in the depths of the rainforest. There had to be some civilization at the other end, wherever that was. And then the sun began to set.

A NIGHT IN THE WILD

Seeing the sun start to go down put us on edge. We were all aware of how many hours it had been since we began walking. It felt like our adventure was turning into a storm of danger. The trail had definitely taken us deeper into the dark rainforest. There was not a hotel or beam of light in any direction. The dense green foliage covering and connecting the trees was now almost black.

Suddenly it occurred to me that no one knew where we were. Our decision to explore the Daintree had been a spur-of-the-moment one, discussed only among ourselves. And frankly, we didn't even know our location in this twelve-hundred-kilometer-square piece of wild. Even if we did, I had no ability to read the map and wasn't so sure I could trust my friends' directional skills. In the fading light, we soon wouldn't be able to make out the road ahead.

When you're in such a predicament, you begin to hear things you hadn't before: The shuffling of creatures overhead and underfoot. The slithering of . . . a snake? The whoosh and brush of branches. The rush of running water. Running water? We had come to a river. Should we follow it along the bank? Or go across? Deciding there was no other way forward, we chose to go through the river to the other side.

We stood at the bank a moment, hesitating. I think the same thought crossed each of our minds: *Are we really going to try to cross a river? What kinds of creatures are lurking in the water? Shouldn't we turn back? But we've come so far already. Surely, we aren't far from some help.*

Mick, who carried the video camera that we'd brought to record our adventure, announced we had about thirty minutes of battery life left—significant because the camera's floodlight was our only source of light.

Thirty minutes? We'd been walking for hours. Thirty minutes wouldn't be nearly enough time. The dark was falling fast. Already it was so dim that I couldn't see entirely across the river.

We looked at one another and nodded. Now, we decided, would be a good time to turn on the camera. We needed light to guide us across the river.

Mick flipped the switch on.

The beams cut through the darkness and illuminated our progress. There were towering trees covered in vines and wild plants. In every direction. As far as we could see. And silhouetted in the background were mountain peaks reaching into an endless sky of distant stars.

We looked at each other, then quickly away again. It was almost unbearable to admit we were lost.

HELPLESS AND HOPELESS

It was only when the light illuminated the darkness that I realized the seriousness of our situation and just how hopelessly lost we really were.

The facts were plain. We'd plunged deep into the wild of the Daintree. It was night. We were on foot with poor shoes. We were without food or water, without protective clothing, without a guidebook, without a cell phone, and without a clue as to where civilization was and how to get back to it.

How foolish we've been, I thought. No one was looking for us. And even when we turned up missing, no one would have any idea where to look. We were novices, tourists out for a fun summer vacation ride, city people with no idea of what we'd just exposed ourselves to, and we were in one of the oldest rainforests in the world, home to venomous snakes, lizards, and spiders. Even without those odds, my idea of camping was more like slow room service than sleeping in a tent or under stars on the mossy ground at the base of a tree.

Just a day earlier, this would have been a joke, but we weren't laughing now. It's not that we were terrified. We probably should have been *more* scared than we were. But we did realize that we needed help. We'd gotten ourselves into a terrible situation, and none of us knew how we were going to get out.

With the battery burning, we braced ourselves to cross the river. Silently we stepped, single file, into the water. The river was shallow enough that we could cross by walking, but it was freezing cold. I forced myself to keep moving, to stay focused on getting across. The boys helped Kylie, Sally, and me as we struggled for footing in our flip-flops. I so wanted to freak out—the camera's stark light revealed cockroaches on the banks—but I kept praying my way across.

As if on cue, just as we all reached the far bank, the light of the video camera went out.

How eerie and yet comforting at the same time, I thought. *Thank you, God,* I prayed. *You saw us through. Now please see us safely home.* Though we had no idea what was ahead, God had seen us through what I was sure would be the worst of our wandering. Surely.

Adjusting to the pitch black, we appreciated the little bit of moonlight that guided us. Silently, we walked through the fringes of vines and branches. We began to hear little pings and patters. Rain. The scent of the storm, which might have seemed pleasantly fragrant earlier, came on strong and signaled more trouble. I looked at my watch as the downpour set in: one in the morning. It had been twelve hours since lunch. I was beginning to feel the effects of dehydration. My mouth felt so dry, like I'd been chewing cotton balls. My stomach was angry, growling for food. The rest of my body was chilled. The rain added more than discomfort. In my shorts and T-shirt, I shivered. I was slightly light-headed, finding it difficult to focus. I no longer wondered if we'd get back in time to catch our flight home. I began to wonder how we would get back at all.

"We've got to stop," Sally said. She looked as sick as I felt.

It was too dark to proceed anyway. We looked for some shelter where we could rest until dawn. Though there were trees everywhere—this was the rainforest!—none of them seemed to offer a ceiling from the storm. We hunted for fallen branches and loose sticks to fashion into a shelter. We finally huddled together under our excuse for a lean-to against a massive tree. I rubbed my hands and feet. Prickly vines, spiny bushes, and other vegetation had cut and bruised my tired limbs. I felt dirty, fatigued, hungry, thirsty—and hopeless. We were undoubtedly all thinking the same thing: *None of us knows how to get out of this mess.*

Exhausted, we dozed, often jerking awake with pain or cold. We nodded off deeply into our own thoughts, mostly of our loved ones back home, knowing they had no idea that we were lost in the rainforest instead of asleep in our hotel beds, packed for tomorrow's flight home.

Not one other human being on earth knows our trouble, I thought. *But you know, God. Could you somehow rescue us from this mess we've gotten ourselves into? I'm sorry we were so irresponsible. I know this is no one's fault but our own. We have no one to blame but ourselves. We've been unwise, and this is our consequence. But help us, God. Please, please help us.*

Five miserable hours later, the sun rose. Once again, the light illuminated the desperation of our situation. We were filthy and mud-caked. Our eyes bloodshot with dark circles underneath from exhaustion. Though the rain had stopped, we were soaked and aching. Sally and Paul couldn't even walk. They had cut their feet so badly gathering sticks and branches before we'd climbed under the tree, their feet were now swollen and too sore. I felt the sting of every one of my own cuts on my legs, hands, and feet.

For another hour, we sat nursing ourselves, evaluating every possible course of action. Keep walking forward? We had no idea what was ahead, and we were feeling weaker rather than stronger. Wait where we were? We could be waiting here for weeks. No one was looking for us, and what were the chances of someone venturing along? Maybe we should try to go back. But then, we'd come so far. Going back would take at least another day, maybe two, considering our deteriorating physical state. Every option seemed a dead end.

"Enough," Mick said finally. "I'm making an executive decision. I feel strong. I'm going ahead for help. The rest of you should wait here. You'd only slow me down anyway. I'll send help back for you."

Though none of us said it, the rest were surely thinking what I was: *Not likely*. Even so, Mick was right. We had to do something. If we all just sat there, we would inevitably die. Feeling grim and scared, we reluctantly agreed. But first, we decided, the rest of us should move to higher ground. There was a cliff nearby. We would perch on its edge.

"The chances of you finding us again are better that way," Paul told Mick, "if you're successful."

That *if* weighed heavily on our minds.

From our new, higher vantage point, Paul, Kylie, Sally, and I watched Mick retreat into the forest, and then we fell into silence, again adrift in our own thoughts.

I sat on the wet ground, pulling my knees up to my chin and hugging my legs. The pressure of limb against limb slightly eased the sting of my cuts. But my bruises from the slide in the Jeep and our push through the underbrush began to ache all over again.

Over the next five hours, we each fidgeted every time a branch twitched or bush crackled in the forest. At ten that morning, I thought of our plane taking off, returning to Sydney. The flight was three hours, and only when we didn't disembark would anyone think to try to contact us. They would trace us to the hotel, where we had not yet checked out, but no one would know where we had gone. They wouldn't even know where to begin to look. How would they find us in this wild, dense rainforest? Our Jeep was as lost to the world as we were, hidden deep in the forest, off the road and down a mountainside. Surely the night's rains had washed away even the evidence of our slide as well as any of our footprints.

Another four hours passed. My stomach ached for food, and though it was the middle of the day, I was shivering. Our exposure to the elements was taking its toll. I worried about Mick. What if he hurt himself? Or encountered some dangerous animal? My mind was having trouble focusing, and I slipped into despair. It would take a miracle to get us out of this situation. Things would only grow worse: the hunger, the hurt, the fatigue.

I began to give up any hope of being rescued.

Slowly, hurting with each step, I gathered some palm and fern leaves to make myself a deathbed. I spread them out and lay carefully on them, eyes closed, arms folded across my chest.

"What are you doing?" Paul asked.

"If we're found, I want to look peaceful," I said.

"Chris, you are such a drama queen," Kylie said.

She was right, but I also genuinely believed that this probably was the very end. I had always wondered how I would feel when this moment came, and I was somewhat surprised at how calm I felt. I thought about my family and all my relationships and my life up to this point. *God,* I prayed, *I am so grateful that you saved me and allowed me to serve you, but I really didn't think I would come home like this. I thought you had so much more for me. At least I know I really do believe in you, Lord, and I'm ready to meet you face-to-face. Please be with my mum and family and team as they deal with this. Lord, I am so sorry we were so careless. I know we should have been more careful, but I can't change that now.*

Then suddenly, as I was praying out my final epitaph, Kylie jolted me. "Do you hear that?" she whispered, breathless.

"What?" Paul asked.

I listened.

"Don't you hear?" she insisted.

All I heard was Kylie rustling, trying to stand. *She's delirious,* I thought. *How nice, God, for you to give her a hallucination to get her through the passing from this life to the next.*

Then I felt a slight vibration, a tremor in the trees, on the ground, followed by the sound of a steady, beating whir. I rubbed my ears. The sound didn't go away. It was getting louder. I felt a force of air and opened one eye.

Kylie and Paul were standing, waving madly at the sky, shouting, "Here! We're here!" Their shouts and an even stronger rush of air made me sit up and look around to see. It was a helicopter! Mick was leaning out from the side of it as it hovered just above us. He too waved, beaming.

I jumped up and ran to the cliff's edge. I will never forget standing there on that precipice, yelling, "We're saved! We're saved! We're saved!" Overjoyed. Relieved. Incredulously happy. We had been so lost, and now we were found! I wanted to express all my excitement in every way possible. But instead I froze. Not because of the sharp drop over the cliff's edge or my sore feet and aching limbs. But because of the words I sensed in my heart, that flooded my mind, that became direction for my life. *Yes, Christine, you are saved. Remember what it is to be saved. Remember what it was to be lost. Remember the darkness and the difference between feeling carefree one morning and by evening sad and scared and sorry for being careless. Remember that I am here. Remember that I want to save every soul. And remember what it is to be unable on your own ability to get out of the dark.*

Then a ladder dropped down from the sky. I blinked up into what was startling light after our dark night and day of the soul. As I grabbed onto the first rung, it was like grabbing God's hand, and it filled me with gratitude. In the bright light, I thought, *I will never forget.* How could I? A minute before, I was utterly hopeless, preparing to die, feeling forgotten and far from help, beyond rescue, in such a strange and unforgiving place, surrounded by predators, aching and cut, sore and soaked by rain, fear, and despair.

The rescue team dropped a safety cable, and I wrapped the harness around my waist. I climbed up the ladder rungs, dangling there above the wild, where moments ago I'd expected to die. How different the rainforest looked in the light of hope. *Just trees,* I remember thinking. *Just trees.* Above, the rescue team was ready to pull me safely into the helicopter. Once inside, I marveled at the change made by the hand that reached out to rescue me. I even laughed, because I couldn't help but think how this seemed more like a scene in some TV series than an actual experience in my life.

I looked around at my friends, one by one crawling safely inside the helicopter. The rescue team had dropped everything and gone to great expense to look for us, find us, and bring us out of the dark and danger. It was sobering to realize: *Saving costs something. Rescuing risks everything.*

And that's exactly what God did for us by sending Jesus into the world to seek and save that which was lost.[1]

As I undid the safety harness, I looked up to heaven and whispered a promise. "God, I will not forget those still lost in the darkness."

WE WEREN'T THE FIRST TO BE LOST

I will never forget that feeling of being lost. I had never known it like that before. And yet, in the days after we were rescued, it was so tempting to go back to life as usual. To forget what it felt like to be hopeless. Helpless. Not knowing if we would ever be found. I yearned for normalcy, to go on with my life, but Jesus didn't want me to forget.

I believe that's why Jesus told story after story about how easy it is to be lost and how remarkable it is to be saved. He doesn't want any of us to forget. Jesus told stories of people hopeless and hurting. People who needed living water, whose souls were tattered, who felt like the dark was closing in on them and time was running out.

There's a chapter in the Bible, Luke 15, where Jesus tells three stories—one of a lost sheep, then a lost coin, and finally a lost son. Three stories. One chapter. All about something lost. I believe God was wanting to get across to us three very important points about how he sees the lost and how he wants us to see them too. How he wants us to remember them—always—in whatever he's called us to do.

As the chapter begins, Jesus teaches by telling about a lost sheep and the profound actions of the shepherd who went to find him. "Suppose one of you has a hundred sheep and loses one of them. Doesn't he leave the ninety-nine in the open country and go after the lost sheep until he finds it? And when he finds it, he joyfully puts it on his shoulders and goes home. Then he calls his friends and neighbors together and says, 'Rejoice with me; I have found my lost sheep.' I tell you that in the same way there will be more rejoicing in heaven over one sinner who repents than over ninety-nine righteous persons who do not need to repent."[2]

Jesus was telling us how much the one matters. That even if you have one hundred sheep and one wanders away, you go after the one. One is as valuable as ninety-nine. The implication is that not one sheep—not one person—is insignificant.

How could an almighty God do any less? Can you imagine what his message to us would be otherwise? "I'll come after you and save you *if* I'm not too busy saving others and *if* my attention isn't needed keeping the ninety-nine others safe. After all, you probably got into this mess yourself, and it wouldn't be fair to deprive the others, who are being good, of my time and attention just to keep coming after you. I'll help you if circumstances allow. Otherwise you're on your own."

Never in Scripture does Jesus give a message anything like this. Instead he promises to come after the one, because each of us is precious to him. I remember thinking how the helicopter that came to find us in the rainforest targeted us five to rescue. They focused on just us and not the other twenty-four million people in Australia that day. That's how Jesus comes seeking the lost. Everyone matters to him. Every one.

In the next story—the story of the lost coin—Jesus continues teaching, helping us realize that just as a coin doesn't lose itself, it's not always our fault when we get lost. "Or suppose a woman has ten silver coins and loses one. Doesn't she light a lamp, sweep the house and search carefully until she finds it? And when she finds it, she calls her friends and neighbors together and says, 'Rejoice with me; I have found my lost coin.' In the same way, I tell you, there is rejoicing in the presence of the angels of God over one sinner who repents."[3]

Was the woman so busy that she forgot where she'd placed the coin? Did she take her eyes off her treasure for only a moment, and a thief snatched it? Did she trip, spilling all her coins onto the floor, where one rolled out of sight? Did a debt or an addiction cause her to gamble away part of her money and then even more, in a desperate attempt to win it back?

Some people are lost not because of something they willfully did but through no fault of their own, because of a place they fell into, because of circumstances they couldn't control. They may be lost because when they were just a child, the words of an insensitive adult stung them, or they endured the neglect of an absent parent, even the malice of a physical or emotional abuser. I was abandoned as an infant, left unwanted, unnamed in a hospital, adopted by loving parents but abused for years at the hands of broken men. I never fit into my big Greek family culture because I liked to read instead of cook, play soccer instead of dance ballet. I was rejected by my peers, teased because of my ethnicity. They saw me as different—a Greek, someone from an immigrant family who didn't belong. I was lost on so many levels.

What all lost people have in common, no matter how it is they came to be lost, is that they have lost their purpose, passion, or potential, even their destiny. They've lost their way.

Who is God calling you to reach out to? Who have you encountered that didn't mean to get lost? I know it can be scary to reach out to someone others have been careless with—the homeless, the immigrant, the addict. I understand how we can fear the lost, whoever they are, and how we can be intimidated by them. I understand how we can be afraid of their rejection, their judgment, their power to affect our position or well-being. How we can be unsure what to do, because they're needy and desperate. We don't know if they will attach themselves to us and beg for one thing after another—our time, our money, our emotional support that we aren't sure we can fully give—so we fear them.

Sometimes we fear others simply because they are different from us. They have a different lifestyle, culture, and language. They dress differently, eat foods we've never tried, listen to music we've never heard, or joke in a way we don't understand. And rather than run to them, we pull back, wondering whether they will accept us. Will they laugh at us behind our backs? Will they despise us even as we sacrifice for them? Are they, perhaps, even a danger to us? Might they be willing to take by force those things we don't offer freely? Will we feel uncomfortable, uneasy, in their midst?

LOVE GOES AFTER THE LOST

The third story Jesus told is one about a prodigal son who had been given everything—not only his father's resources but also his heart and blessing—and then squandered it all, descending into humiliation and poverty.

Jesus continued: "There was a man who had two sons. The younger one said to his father, 'Father, give me my share of the estate.' So he divided his property between them.

"Not long after that, the younger son got together all he had, set off for a distant country and there squandered his wealth in wild living. After he had spent everything, there was a severe famine in that whole country, and he began to be in need. So he went and hired himself out to a citizen of that country, who sent him to his fields to feed pigs. He longed to fill his stomach with the pods that the pigs were eating, but no one gave him anything.

"When he came to his senses, he said, 'How many of my father's hired servants have food to spare, and here I am starving to death! I will set out and go back to my father and say to him: Father, I have sinned against heaven and against you. I am no longer worthy to be called your son; make me like one of your hired servants.' So he got up and went to his father.

"But while he was still a long way off, his father saw him and was filled with compassion for him; he ran to his son, threw his arms around him and kissed him.

"The son said to him, 'Father, I have sinned against heaven and against you. I am no longer worthy to be called your son.'

"But the father said to his servants, 'Quick! Bring the best robe and put it on him. Put a ring on his finger and sandals on his feet. Bring the fattened calf and kill it. Let's have a feast and celebrate. For this son of mine was dead and is alive again; he was lost and is found.' So they began to celebrate.

"Meanwhile, the older son was in the field. When he came near the house, he heard music and dancing. So he called one of the servants and asked him what was going on. 'Your brother has come,' he replied, 'and your father has killed the fattened calf because he has him back safe and sound.'

"The older brother became angry and refused to go in. So his father went out and pleaded with him. But he answered his father, 'Look! All these years I've been slaving for you and never disobeyed your orders. Yet you never gave me even a young goat so I could celebrate with my friends. But when this son of yours who has squandered your property with prostitutes comes home, you kill the fattened calf for him!'

"'My son,' the father said, 'you are always with me, and everything I have is yours. But we had to celebrate and be glad, because this brother of yours was dead and is alive again; he was lost and is found.'"[4]

The father was willing to overlook his son's transgressions because he was so glad to have back the son he loved so much. But let's face it, many of us secretly feel, as did the older brother in the story, that the younger son had made his own mess and ought to suffer the consequences for it.

No, Jesus says. The squandering son is as important and beloved as the dutiful older brother—as is the little lost lamb too preoccupied with lunch to keep up with the flock, and the money misplaced by circumstance. Why do we sometimes feel that the seriously, deeply lost should be on their own, that they got themselves into dire straits of their own volition and should get themselves out or stay that way?

No, Jesus says. The one is as important as the ninety-nine.

Maybe the one is a single mom whose income pays only some of the bills and who is maxing out her credit cards to cover the rest of her family's necessities.

Maybe the one is the couple working so hard at their jobs and managing their home that they're drifting apart, and the intimacy of their marriage is slipping away.

Maybe the one is the CEO who has worked her way to the top of the corporate ladder but is experiencing such dissatisfaction and malaise that she's wondering whether that ladder is leaning against the right wall.

What if the one is someone who has lived a life of crime that has landed him in jail?

What if the one is someone who has willfully hurt another?

What if the one is selfish, addicted, immoral, or arrogant? What if he or she is a mocker, a scoffer, a murderer, or a prostitute?

If our example is Jesus, a Savior who stood up for a woman caught in adultery, a greedy, dishonest tax collector, even a thief on a cross,[5] then we won't try to distinguish between the one who is lost because of circumstances beyond his control and the one who willfully put himself there.

Think of it this way: When someone is trapped in a burning building, we don't try to work out what caused the fire and then decide whether the people inside get our sympathy. When people are in danger of burning up, we rush to save them. Especially if we remember how much it hurts to be burned.

No matter how the treasure of a soul comes to be lost, our job is to go and rescue and save what is precious, and in these three stories, Jesus is making it clear to us what is precious. The one who is just like you. Just like me.

Jesus is teaching us something he wants us to always remember:

"The Son of Man came to seek and to save the lost."[6] He came for us and we must go to others, whether or not they realize they are lost, and no matter how they got lost in the first place. When the helicopter came to get us in the Daintree, I knew I was lost, but I had no idea how lost until I looked at a map later and realized the distance between where we entered the rainforest and where we were found. I'm so glad the rescue team didn't ignore us just because our inexperience and poor decisions landed us in such a vulnerable place of being lost and feeling so hopeless and helpless. I'm so glad they understood that their mission is always to rescue the lost.

I HAVE NEVER FORGOTTEN

To this day, I've never forgotten God's charge to me: *Remember what it is to be saved. Remember what it was to be lost.* That's what I was remembering in Thessaloniki that day when I met with the girls, when Sonia asked, "Why didn't you come sooner?" I fiercely sought to be undaunted for her, to answer her with the words Jesus would want me to say. To remember what God wanted me never to forget.

I know that for the desperate, the hungry, the oppressed, for those in pain, no rescue can come soon enough. And when the lost call to us for rescue, God doesn't command us to do anything except to be willing and to move forward undaunted. To trust that as we step out in faith, he will do what only he can do. He will save that which was lost.[7]

The helicopter pilot and crew who came to get us that day risked it all. It was a dangerous mission with no guarantees. But they came.

As the church, it's time for us to go. We are the rescue crew that God has deployed to join him in the greatest rescue mission of all time.

I don't know what God has called you to do, but I do know there are people he never wants you to forget as you fulfill your calling. He wants you to race past your hesitation, reach beyond your discomfort, and forget your inadequacy. There are so, so many people he wants you to help rescue. People like we all once were. Lost.

Chapter 8

HE DIDN'T GIVE ME A CAGED LIFE

———⟨∞∞∞⟩———

Sitting in silence, I couldn't take my eyes off the male lion. Waking up slowly, he seemed indifferent to our presence, yet I could tell he was very aware that we were there, watching him from the safety of our open-air vehicle. He raised his head high, shaking his thick mane. His cavernous yawn seemed only to exaggerate his disregard. Yet I could tell he never truly let go of his watchfulness.

I had never been on a safari before, and seeing a lion for the first time outside of a zoo was captivating. Nick and I were in South Africa for a speaking engagement when our hosts learned about my obsession with *The Lion King* movie and graciously organized this adventure of a lifetime for us. They had no idea it was a dream come true for me.

Knowing the lion wouldn't be alone, our guide directed our gaze to the vast plain that stretched for miles. Peering through binoculars, hoping for a sighting, we caught a glimpse of two females, heads bobbing through the tall grasses. In the predawn light, we began to make out even younger yet fully grown lions as well. Most likely they were hunting, our guide explained. Imagining what they

might find for breakfast—a springbok, an antelope, or even a wilde-
beest—I shuddered, thinking of the animal who might not get away.

We had risen while it was still dark so that we could see as
many animals as possible before they took to the shade of the bush
and escaped the heat of the day. We drove throughout the beautiful
preserve on dirt roads, across rivers, underneath thickets. Every
place we explored was teeming with wildlife. Listening to our guide
describe the different bird sounds, straining to distinguish their
screeching, hooting, and cuckooing, I found myself mesmerized,
appreciating their wonderful chorus. I marveled at the giraffes and
zebras and their elegant gallops. What perfectly painted creatures
God had made. Even the rhinos and hyenas seemed beautiful to me
in such a natural setting.

Never had I seen so many animals in a place of such freedom.
And seeing the lions, right before the sun's full rise, was the most
spectacular moment of our entire trip. I'll always remember watching that male lion when he finally stood. Weighing more than
four hundred pounds, he was the real lion king. Untamed, undo-
mesticated, wild. There was an air about him. No wonder we call
courageous people lionhearted. I felt sure he had no fear.

CAGED AND NOT FREE

Leaving our adventure behind a few days later, we headed home to
Sydney. Friends from overseas were coming to visit, and we planned
to take them and their family to the Taronga Zoo. The irony of our
plans didn't escape me, and I wondered if a trip to the zoo would
ever be as fun to me again. Probably not, but time with friends and
watching my girls' fascination with "wild" animals would be a treat.

A couple of days after our friends' arrival, when they had recov-
ered from their jet lag, we set out for our day at the zoo. Walking
the manicured and paved paths, we passed all the animals native
to Australia—the koalas, kangaroos, and emus. I love that the red
kangaroo and the emu are pictured on the Australian coat of arms.

They are two of only three animals that can only move forward, the direction God wants us to go.

When we reached the petting zoo, the kids all emptied our pockets of change so they could buy morsels of food out of the vending machines to feed the animals. It was all a far cry from our safari experience, but it was great fun. Coming upon the giraffe enclosure, we basked in the expansive panorama. High atop a hill, the giraffes have the best view of the Sydney Harbour Bridge and the Sydney Opera House. Watching our friends and all the kids experiencing the giraffes' spectacular vantage point, it was hard not to appreciate the wonders of the zoo.

Strolling on through the park, meandering past animals I had seen in the wild only a week or so before, I couldn't help but think of them differently. Zebras. Elephants. Hippos. Once I had never given any thought to their contentment or well-being; I now felt like a protective conservator questioning everything about them. Had they been caught and brought here? Had they been born in captivity? Did they innately know the difference? Did they know they were supposed to be wild, or did they just accept their caged life as the bane of their existence?

I supposed they didn't really think about any of that. After all, they were animals. But I couldn't stop thinking about it.

Lost in my musings, mindlessly following our group from exhibit to exhibit, I was surprised to realize we had navigated our way right into the middle of the African lion exhibit. Peering through the security fence and across the dry moat, trying not to compare the lions with the ones I'd seen on safari, I was taken aback by their complacent demeanor. Instead of merely looking at them, appreciating their impressive size and presence, especially so up close, I found myself feeling agitated, even more concerned about them than I had been about the zebras or elephants. I felt my heart ache at the noticeable difference between these lions and the lions I'd seen in the South African wild.

Instead of shaking off my introspections, I found myself going even deeper. Something was not right. Something was amiss, far beyond the realization that some animals live in the wild and some live in a zoo. Still staring at the lions, trying to understand what was tugging at my mind and my heart, I watched how they behaved. Tame. Domesticated. Caged. They certainly didn't appear watchful, alert, or assertive. They didn't care at all about any of the visitors staring at them, calling out to them, or the children running around their enclosure to get a better view.

As I watched the lions pace the perimeter of their habitat, I knew God was showing me something significant. Turning to Nick, I began to talk about what I was sensing.

God created these lions to roam free on the savanna, not to live caged in a zoo. And he created us to live the same way. He found us when we were lost and saved us. He made us free to roam, to run, to seek him and all the plans and purpose he has for our lives. Jesus came to give us an abundant life, not a meager one.[1]

But somewhere along the way, life happens to all of us. We get lured into a place that is small and contained, and we settle for it. We opt to live a smaller story. Like the lions, we live caged in plain sight. And we accept it. Confined by our fears, insecurities, and hurts. Limited by rejection we've endured, by bitterness that takes hold of us, or by unforgiveness we don't know how to resolve. Stifled by culture, tradition, even well-intentioned religion. Despite what we say we want, deep down we're hesitant, afraid even, to live the full, abundant life Jesus came to give us.

But unlike the lions, we have a choice.

What if I'd never dealt with my fears? What if I'd given in to them and let them decide my future? I'd be grounded, limited to only the places I could get to by car or train. I'd be just like these lions, lured into believing that a controlled life is better than a wild one. Lured into a place where I'd never get the chance to fulfill all that God has planned for me. I never want to be a lion in a zoo. I want to run free on the plains. I want to go after everything God has called me to do.

Nick, understanding my every word, nodded thoughtfully and smiled. Equally as passionate about the life God had called us to live together, we stood shoulder to shoulder in silence, watching four playful cubs run around and over their protective mother. They were nipping one another, chasing one another, lost in the freedom that comes with the feeling of complete trust.

I kept thinking. As happy as those lion cubs were, most likely having been born into captivity, even they had been made for something far bigger. They just didn't know it. I thought of how the apostle Paul challenged the Corinthians with this very idea. "Dear, dear Corinthians, I can't tell you how much I long for you to enter this wide-open, spacious life. We didn't fence you in. The smallness you feel comes from within you. Your lives aren't small, but you're living them in a small way. I'm speaking as plainly as I can and with great affection. Open up your lives. Live openly and expansively!"[2]

I wanted to live God's wide-open, spacious life more than ever! To walk in faith, fully trusting in where he would lead. Standing there in front of the lion cages, I committed anew in my heart to live the life God had planned for me. I didn't want to miss one adventure, one assignment, one person. Not one.

I wanted to live my life with the kind of faith God has given all of us, one that by its very nature is unsafe and unlimited. One that is out of my control and under his. One that is wild, routed through all the unexplored, unchartered, unknown, unsettled places where he wants me to go. If it were any different, then it wouldn't be faith. It wouldn't be faith if there were no risk. It wouldn't be faith if it was predictable. Controllable. Containable.

After all, the Bible describes faith as the substance of things hoped for, the confidence, assurance, evidence of things *not seen*.[3] It takes faith to believe in something before one sees it, to genuinely walk by faith and not by sight.[4] One translation even describes faith as "the firm foundation . . . that makes life worth living."[5]

That was the life I wanted.

CHOOSE GOD'S WIDE-OPEN, SPACIOUS LIFE

Moving into the wide-open, spacious life God has called us to—a life of faith—will always be our choice to make. In the animal kingdom, lions can be captured and rehomed in a zoo, forced to leave one habitat and adapt to another, but God will never force us to exchange one life for another. He calls us to a life of undaunted faith, but whether we live it will always be our choice.[6]

Life will always throw us curveballs. We will all be blindsided by challenges, failures, losses, hurts, betrayals—distractions of every kind—and each time, we will be free to choose whether to settle for a caged life or move into a free one. When I learned that I was adopted—abandoned by my birth mother at a hospital, given a number instead of a name, and then adopted by loving parents who kept this secret from me for thirty-three years—I could have succumbed to a caged life, letting the pain of my past lock me up and keep me confined forever. But I had a choice. I could let the shock of it all cause me to spiral downward into captivity mentally, emotionally, even physically, or I could walk in faith. I chose to put my trust in God and keep moving forward with undaunted faith, though at times it felt like more than I could bear. Moving through hurt or pain is never easy.

When God began opening doors for me to speak outside of Australia, to visit places that required a flight, I could have said no. No to flying. No to God. No to my calling. And as I told you, at first I did! But God helped me overcome my fear. I kept moving forward in faith, and now I'm not afraid to fly anywhere!

Each time God showed me a place in my heart where I was caged in—whether it was because of something done to me or a consequence of my actions—I chose to break out and move forward. To move into his spacious life. To live the bigger life that he had planned. Whatever God had called me to do, I wanted to go for it. I wanted to help others. To lead them to Christ. I didn't want to get stuck and forfeit my calling.

But each time it took faith. Just like I've written about in chapter after chapter.

It took faith to understand my parents' decision to keep my adoption a secret.

It took faith to forgive the men who abused me.

It took faith to move through the sorrow of losing a baby and then have Sophia.

It took faith to deal with my fear of flying and cramped spaces.

It took faith to keep moving into each new wide-open place God showed me, to keep daring to fulfill whatever he was calling me to do in the face of the pain, fears, challenges, and obstacles life kept throwing my way. And it will take that same kind of undaunted faith for you to move into your future.

Undaunted doesn't mean it will be painless.

Undaunted doesn't mean you will never feel betrayed.

Undaunted doesn't mean you will never be fearful.

Undaunted doesn't mean you will never grow weary.

Undaunted doesn't mean you will never fail.

Undaunted doesn't mean you will never be disappointed.

Undaunted doesn't mean you will never be confused.

Undaunted means that despite all these feelings, we trust, knowing that he who promised is faithful, that because greater is he who is in us than he who is in the world, we have the strength to walk by faith every step of every day.[7]

ONE MORE NIGHT WITH THE FROGS

Whatever God has called us to do, no doubt, it will take faith. It takes faith to step out of our comfort zone when we do not feel ready. It takes faith to build a business unlike anything we've ever done before. It takes faith to finish school, go back to school, or launch a new career. It takes faith to move forward even while we still feel afraid. It takes faith to think of others and not just ourselves.

It takes faith to rock the status quo. It takes faith to not settle for less than God's best.

It especially takes faith to deal with the issues that keep us caged and living a smaller life, the kind that hold us back from our future. The kind that pop up from our past, putting a damper on our present. The kind that work their way into our current narrative from unexpected experiences—losing a job, our marriage, or our home. The kind that silently stalk our thinking and shape our perspectives, lulling us into believing lies—that we aren't good enough, that we can't succeed, that we aren't qualified, or that it's too risky to move outside the zone where we feel safe and secure.

To break out of our cages, to move forward, we must decide to start confronting the issues holding us back today. We cannot wait until the planets align, until all our circumstances are changed, or until we feel like it. We must move now. Act now. Go now.

And yet the temptation to hesitate will always be there. Our humanity will always pull on us to postpone. To stay stuck, caged right where we are.

In the book of Exodus, there is a fascinating story about the consequences of waiting—of procrastinating—when we should be moving. It's a story that has always struck me as so random because it's a story about frogs! Yes, frogs. Those slimy, hopping, croaking, cold, wet amphibians. The ones my daughters and I don't like, don't want to hold, and certainly don't want anywhere near us. I don't know exactly why God chose to put a story about frogs in the Bible. He certainly has a vast imagination, and the outrageous events he orchestrated in the Bible never, ever make for boring stories. And this frog one—it doesn't disappoint.

When the frog story begins in the book of Exodus, the Israelites—also known as the Hebrews—had been serving as slave labor for the Egyptians for approximately four hundred years. Three million strong, they were forced to work as brick masons and builders and to perform all kinds of work in the fields. They served to support the Egyptian infrastructure. And God wanted to free them and lead them to the promised land.

So God called Moses, a man who had been born a Hebrew but was raised by an Egyptian princess, to appeal to Pharaoh to let the Hebrews go. When Moses went before him, Pharaoh refused— repeatedly. He was hard-hearted and a cruel taskmaster. To soften Pharaoh's heart and persuade him to let the people go, God began sending plagues, eventually ten in all. And the frogs were the second plague to consume the land. "Then the LORD said to Moses, 'Go to Pharaoh and say to him, "This is what the LORD says: Let my people go, so that they may worship me. If you refuse to let them go, I will send a plague of frogs on your whole country.""'[8]

Frogs. What a surprise! I've tried to imagine the look on Pharaoh's face when he heard the word *frogs*. I doubt that it was fear. After all, frogs are not daunting creatures. Unpleasant, maybe. Kind of gross to many of us, but not dangerous, vicious, or deadly. I wonder if Pharaoh scoffed, wrinkled his nose in disgust, raised an eyebrow in surprise. Maybe he laughed. We can only imagine. But when Moses continued, he left nothing to Pharaoh's imagination. Moses spelled out exactly what Egypt would experience. "The Nile will teem with frogs. They will come up into your palace and your bedroom and onto your bed, into the houses of your officials and on your people, and into your ovens and kneading troughs. The frogs will come up on you and your people and all your officials."[9]

No part of their lives, including the spaces where they worked, slept, even prepared their food and ate, would remain unaffected. Every person in Egypt would have to deal with the effects of this plague, rich and poor, commoners and palace officials alike. The frogs would be inescapable. But Pharaoh didn't yield. "Then the LORD said to Moses, 'Tell Aaron, "Stretch out your hand with your staff over the streams and canals and ponds, and make frogs come up on the land of Egypt."' So Aaron stretched out his hand over the waters of Egypt, and the frogs came up and covered the land."[10]

The next verse cracks me up. Pharaoh still didn't get it, and neither did his magicians. They seemed to think they were in a frog-making contest with the God of Moses! "But the magicians did the same things by their secret arts; they also made frogs come up on the land of Egypt."[11]

As if a kingdom full of frogs weren't enough to deal with, the magicians made even more! And while they were concentrating on their competition with God, they were blind to the consequences of a major frog invasion.

But I can't be too critical of them. After all, that was me in my pre-sold-out-to-Jesus years! I lived through them with such brokenness. Rather than run to God for healing and wholeness, I allowed what had been done to me to slime my life for years. I was afraid, so I ran away from God, not knowing he was:

- the one wanting to heal me and make me whole
- the one wanting to free me to be who he created me to be, and empower me to do what he created me to do
- the one wanting to reveal to me a calling for me to pursue— for my good, for others' good, and for his glory
- the one wanting me to learn how to live with wild faith, undaunted

Like Pharaoh's magicians, I made more slime.

Eventually, it dawned on Pharaoh that life with frogs was exceedingly unpleasant. We don't know what triggered this realization. Was it when he slipped into a warm bath that night and discovered that sharing it with frogs made for a miserable soak? Was it the stench of sizzling frogs wafting up from the palace ovens? Was it when Mrs. Pharaoh ran screeching from her bed because of the frogs between the sheets, announcing that either the frogs had to go or she would? Whatever the turning point, he was finally so overwhelmed by the plague of frogs that he swallowed his pride. "Pharaoh summoned Moses and Aaron and said, 'Pray to the LORD to take the frogs away from me and my people, and I will let your people go to offer sacrifices to the LORD.'"[12]

The stalemate was broken. The showdown over. Pharaoh was so sick and tired of wall-to-wall frogs that he finally asked for God's help.

I've been there. Have you? So desperate to get out of a mess that we're finally willing to beg God to rescue us from it. It's a moment God seems to always be waiting for us to reach. When we're no longer held back by our insecurities and hurts. By our fear of rejection and failure. When we've grown more daunted by the reality of staying in the cage we've built than by the prospect of moving forward into the wide-open, spacious place God has called us to.

When Pharaoh finally cried uncle, surely all the Egyptians sighed in relief that the frogs would soon be history.

Moses' response was gracious. Rather than gloat or make Pharaoh squirm in humility, he honored Pharaoh with a show of respect. After all, he wasn't there to humiliate Pharaoh, just to win freedom for God's people. He offered Pharaoh a chance to save face. "Moses said to Pharaoh, 'I leave to you the honor of setting the time for me to pray for you and your officials and your people that you and your houses may be rid of the frogs, except for those that remain in the Nile.'"[13]

There it is. God is willing to get rid of the frogs, and he's even willing to offer Pharaoh the courtesy of naming the time. God gives him a choice, just like he always gives us a choice. All Pharaoh has to do is say the word, and the God of Moses will act on his behalf. The moment is his.

"Tomorrow," Pharaoh said.[14]

Wait. What? *Tomorrow?*

Not now? Not this instant?

No. *Tomorrow!*

That's what the verse says. *Tomorrow!* God offered Pharaoh a frog-free palace, frog-free beds and ovens, an entire frog-free kingdom, and he says, "Tomorrow."

What would drive this man to spend one more night with those frogs when frog-free living was within reach? *Wait until tomorrow?* What possessed him to choose another day, another night, overrun with frogs?

It's a question for us all to consider. What causes us to spend one more night with the frogs we have hopping around in our lives? What are the fears, failures, or disappointments that have invaded our lives and taken up residence—some thrust upon us, some of our own making—that we have become so accustomed to, so tolerant of, that even when the God of the universe offers to take them away, we hesitate? Rather than run forward in faith, we choose to delay.

"Tomorrow," we say. "I'll deal with that tomorrow."

THE CHORUS OF CROAKING FROGS

Maybe we need to better understand how badly frogs hold us back so we are caged and limited, not living in the wide-open, spacious place God has called us to. They aren't just slimy and nasty, they're also loud. And when frogs get to croaking, they can sing some very ugly songs. I know because through the years, I've listened to a lot of their croaking, and for a time I thought it sounded better than freedom. I listened to

- the frog of insecurity, who croaks, "But what if I fail? What if they don't like me? What if I say the wrong thing?"
- the frog of self-pity, who sings a song of self-justification: "It isn't fair. Why did they get away with that? Why does this always happen to me?"
- the frog of bitterness, anger, rage, and resentment, who sings the same old repetitious song. His croaking reassures us that we have every reason to still be angry, to withhold our love, to make them pay.
- the frog of lust, of vice, of self-gratification. He lulls us toward the bottle, a pill, our flesh, driving us to soothe our pain or

ease our loneliness or compensate for our longing, even if just for the moment.

- the frog of familiar old places and faces, who lures us back time and time again to the false promise of comfort.
- the frog of fear, who really makes us procrastinate, stall, and avoid, until we croak right along with him: "I always fall short, I always disappoint. I never succeed, never overcome, never make it to the next phase, never stick to my resolve."
- the frog of unforgiveness and offense, who is so subtle he gets us to rehearse the same old stanzas over and over: "She told me this. He called me that. He did this to me. He left me. He failed me. She lied about me. She accused me."

When our most familiar frogs are croaking softly, we forget they are even there. We don't notice their lingering effects on our lives. We grow accustomed to living caged in the small place their symphony leads us to. Even when coworkers and family members, who can clearly see the frog perched atop our head, call us prickly or sensitive or hostile or impatient, we look around and say, "What frog? What anger issue? I'm not angry!"

And when our frogs are croaking loudly, they make *us* jump. We jump from church to church, looking for the one that doesn't have broken people in it. We jump from relationship to relationship, looking to soothe the isolation or fill the void in our hearts. We jump from one bed into another, trying to find love and significance. We jump from job to job, trying to find value and purpose. We jump. We jump. We jump. We search in vain for some source of security, but we don't know what that source is or where to find it.

Though we hate the negative feelings that come with the songs and habits of our croaking frogs, and though we want to fulfill all that God has called us to do, we refuse to banish the frogs from our lives. In some instances, we've grown so attached to our frogs that their croaking chorus seems more like a nighttime lullaby than a noisy invasion. We play with them, making them pets, instead of ridding them from our lives, and we nourish them as we allow them to feast on our very souls.

Is it possible that we have become so daunted by the croaking frogs that we stay trapped in our cage of safe living instead of looking to the future with undaunted faith?

I've been honest about what I've been through—in this book and all my others—yet I have no idea what you've endured. Maybe you've been shocked by blows you never saw coming. A child you can't reach. A spouse who isn't faithful. The loss of a loved one all too soon. Maybe you've been wronged in ways I can't imagine. Sonia was. As were Nadia, Maria, and Anna. Maybe you failed at something. Caused something. God has mercy for that too. But whatever any of us have been through, facing it and all its pain is the way forward. Surrendering it to God is the way to living a spacious life. To living with undaunted faith.

At every juncture when I could have stayed caged in or moved forward into my future—whether because of abandonment and adoption or abuse and rejection—I made a choice. Each time that I grew sick and tired of being robbed of my present joy by my broken past, by habits I'd developed along the way, or by the unhealthy thinking that assaulted my mind, I chose to trust God more. I wanted to flourish, so I chose to press forward with undaunted faith.

When we finally realize what we've been allowing to happen, when our discomfort grows to the point that we want to be rid of the frogs, we have a choice to make: press in now or procrastinate. It's so tempting to respond like Pharaoh did and postpone our future: "I *will* do something about it . . . tomorrow."

Tomorrow I'll forgive.

Tomorrow I'll let go of my anger.

Tomorrow I'll take a step out of my comfort zone.

Tomorrow I'll get help for my addiction.

Tomorrow I'll quit thinking of just myself.

Tomorrow I'll deal with my apathy.

Tomorrow.

Do you know what tomorrow will become? Today. Always today. Whenever we trade today for tomorrow, whenever we put off putting off the thing that is hindering us today, we postpone our future.

We live caged by the decisions we make or actions we take and by the wrongs we have suffered. We talk about our future. We hope for our future. We even complain about our future. But rather than step out of our caged life and into the future that Jesus Christ died and rose again to give us, we put off the change, the new territory, the hard work, the tough choices, the honest confession, the difficult conversation. We put them off until tomorrow.

The only way to claim our future, to step into the calling God has in store for each and every one of us, is to face our issues with undaunted faith. Today.

What is it that you're putting off until tomorrow? What issue is postponing your future? What do you need to face and over-come today?

Rejection?

Disappointment?

Abuse?

Betrayal?

Failure?

Are you defining yourself by what's been done to you?

Or defining yourself by some wrong you've done?

God is ready to rid our lives of frogs, but he leaves it up to us to choose today. Even Pharaoh finally chose to surrender to God. "Moses replied, 'It will be as you say, so that you may know there is no one like the LORD our God. The frogs will leave you and your houses, your officials and your people; they will remain only in the Nile.' After Moses and Aaron left Pharaoh, Moses cried out to the LORD about the frogs he had brought on Pharaoh. And the LORD did what Moses asked. The frogs died in the houses, in the courtyards and in the fields."[15]

God was faithful, even to Pharaoh. How can he not be faith-ful to you?

Today is the day to move out of the cages that confine us and step into the wide-open, spacious life God destined for us to live. "We are His workmanship, created in Christ Jesus for good works, which God prepared beforehand that we should walk in them."[16]

God has chosen us. He has plucked us out of eternity, positioned us in time, and given us gifts and talents for the purpose of serving our generation. He wants us to live beyond ourselves, outside ourselves, serving others until we take our very last breath. He wants us to do his good works on earth. He calls each of us to do *something*. To go in a divine direction and fulfill a purpose on the earth. A plan of his design.

But it will require us to make a choice. To move forward with undaunted faith. Out of the zoo. Out of the cage. And into a wide-open, spacious life.

PART 4

GOD KNOWS MY DESTINY

Chapter 9

I AWAKENED
TO MORE

———— ⦿ ————

W e drove past villagers pitching hay and working their vegetable gardens in idyllic rolling fields under a brilliant blue sky. No one ever would have suspected the ominous darkness awaiting us at the end of the winding road. The stately line of birch trees standing tall on the horizon belied the evil that once hid behind them.

Though it was a sunny day in May—warm, breezy, almost happy—I was somber. Were this same pastoral scene anywhere else, I felt sure I would have been peaceful. Hopeful. Instead I was braced. Prepared in some way, I suppose. I knew that today, despite the budding of spring and the beautiful countryside, I would see a history of horrors. Remnants of a nation. A friend had agreed to come with me to see a place I'd studied since high school and longed to visit. A place I wanted to see for myself. To understand. To comprehend. Though that didn't seem possible for anyone.

As we continued on the narrow road to Auschwitz-Birkenau, the largest of the Nazi concentration and extermination camps located in southern Poland, we became increasingly aware of how foreboding our journey really was. From 1942 until late 1944, transport trains delivered anyone the Schutzstaffel (SS) deemed an inferior race or a threat to the purity and strength of the German nation. They were brought there from all over Nazi-occupied Europe. More than one million people died there. Most of them were gassed; others died from starvation or disease or were worked to death by forced labor or were otherwise executed. Many people were sickened with infectious disease or tormented by medical experiments.[1]

Over the years, I'd read books, seen movies, and visited Holocaust museums in several countries. I even studied German economic history for three years at the University of Sydney. For some reason, I'd always had an overwhelming interest in World War II history, particularly in what happened to the people sent to the death camps. Now I found myself on the same road they had traveled, on my way to what was for many of them a final destination.

As I approached the camp, nothing could have prepared me for how it would feel to pass through such beautiful and serene countryside only to be stopped by a wrought iron arch still standing, still promising lies.

"Arbeit Macht Frei," the sign read. It was the cynical motto of the Germans. "Work Sets You Free." It was no more true as we stepped out of the car than it was during World War II. Despite the sunniness of the day, I couldn't help but feel chilled to my bones. I stared for what seemed an hour, trying to take it in, I suppose, but also out of a kind of reverence and respect. Just seventy years earlier, people streaming in by the hundreds of thousands to their death had been greeted by this false sign of hope.

The camp had been turned into a giant museum, a reminder to the rest of humanity of the horrors that people could inflict upon each other. My friend and I walked under the arch and joined a tour through the brick buildings. Photographs of prisoners in ill-fitting striped pajamas lined the walls, along with photos of Nazis measuring people's heads in an attempt to show biological ethnic differences.

A sickening ache began in my stomach.

Turning a corner, I was arrested by the sight of a large pile of shoes. They had been gathered after the prisoners were told to remove them. There were hundreds of shoes, worn and scuffed, all shapes, all styles and sizes. They were just shoes, and yet they were so much more. I imagined them on the feet of my daughters. I imagined them on my husband, parents, brothers, me. I imagined where those shoes had walked. Probably at the same kinds of places they would have walked if worn by me and the people I knew and loved—work, parties, school, worship, home. And then they had taken the longest walk of all, to this place, only to be taken off one last time, just before their owners stepped into a death chamber.

I stood before those shoes a long time and wept.

When I finally found the strength to move on, I came upon a display of suitcases, all with names on them—some stamped, others embossed, some engraved on metal plates, still others roughly scribbled across the side. I wondered about the people who bore those names, who had carried these cases, probably not knowing where they were going. What belongings had they packed? Had they thrown things together hurriedly, urged along by soldiers with guns and bayonets, or had they packed slowly, in private, agonizing over what to bring and what to leave behind? There were small suitcases, children's suitcases, like those my daughters pack when we travel. Had the children packed their own belongings? A favorite toy? Snacks? A blanket? A pretty dress, a favorite pillow?

I walked to the next display, a huge pile of hair that had been shaved from the heads of the prisoners. Like sheep, the people had been shorn, stripped of the very things that identified them. Garments. Possessions. Hair.

Next, they were relieved of physical aids: eyeglasses, hearing aids, braces, artificial limbs, dental plates. These things were sold by the Germans or used in sundry ways.

These piles of possessions, the ones on display, belonged to only a few of those who'd been transported here, perhaps the last group.

And Auschwitz was only one of the many death camps through-out Nazi-occupied Europe during the five years of World War II. Human life had no value in these places. People were publicly beaten and shot. Six million Jewish people were exterminated because of their ethnicity alone, part of the systematic genocide of the Holocaust.

Though I was seeing all the evidence, and try as I might, I could not comprehend it all.

My friend and I walked outside to get some fresh air. Across the courtyard sat many more brick buildings that we had not yet entered. Each was full of more stories of horror, pain, loss, and injustice. How could one human being do this to another?

Eventually, we walked into the next building, where a display told how each prisoner who came into Auschwitz—who wasn't sent straight to the gas chamber—was registered and had a number tattooed across his or her arm.[2] From that point on, this number became their identity. They were never again to be called by name. The numbers dehumanized them, desensitized the guards to them. How much easier for the guards to ignore suffering when it did not have a name, when it was merely a number. When the humanity they imprisoned were no longer living, breathing human beings. When they fulfilled their plan of crossing each number off from their reams of pages.

My feet felt leaden, my spirit deflated. I shuffled to the next stop, the crematorium, and read a detailed description of how it was fed. I turned to my friend, who bore the same sorrowful look of bewilderment and shock. For a long time, we stood there. We could not talk of it.

NO LONGER DISTANT

For the next hour, we made our way somberly through more of the camp. Soon we came to the train station and tracks, where, for most prisoners, the hell of camp had begun. Cattle cars had stopped here, and when the doors were opened, the people who had been crammed into each one had piled out. They had been shipped, like livestock, from all across Europe. Here at the station, they were separated into lines and herded toward the horrible building we'd just seen.

I couldn't help but think, *What would I have done, stepping into the light from that dark, windowless cattle car? Would I have cowered in fear? How would I have handled the gnaw of hunger growing in my belly? What would it be like to live in the huts full of the stench of human waste, not knowing from one second to the next whether I would live or die, not knowing at what moment the guards might single me out for abuse, extra work, torture, or worse? What would I have thought, seeing the smoke billow from the chimney of the crematorium?*

The helplessness, the despair, the instinct to protect oneself, the suffocating fear—those all became real to me that day.

It's easy to think of the German atrocities as ancient history, but it happened during the lifetimes of my parents and grandparents—and perhaps yours too. How different it felt to stand there and imagine it all, as opposed to reading of it in a book or seeing it on a television or movie screen. I thought of Corrie ten Boom, whose life was depicted in the movie *The Hiding Place*. She was a young Dutch woman, a Christian, who tried to help her sister and others endure but in the end barely survived herself. I thought of Dietrich Bonhoeffer, the German Lutheran pastor who joined the resistance movement during the war to stop more people from being sent to the camps but was arrested and hanged. I thought of Anne Frank and her family hiding for more than two years because they were Jews, eventually being imprisoned along with millions. And I came full circle to where I was standing, thinking of all the arms tattooed here.

Suddenly the accounts of Auschwitz no longer seemed distant, disconnected, or far removed from my life. Every person killed during the Holocaust seemed to crowd around me. Real people, not just numbers. I shuddered, remembering that I too had once been only a number until my parents adopted me and named me.

History always has a context. Thousands and thousands of people shut their eyes and allowed this to happen around them. Erwin Lutzer in his book *When a Nation Forgets God* includes an account from an eyewitness who lived in Germany during the 1930s and 1940s.

> I lived in Germany during the Nazi Holocaust. I considered myself a Christian. We heard stories of what was happening to Jews, but we tried to distance ourselves from it because what could we do to stop it. A railroad track ran behind our small church and each Sunday morning we could hear the whistle in the distance, and then the wheels coming over the tracks. We became disturbed when we heard the cries coming from the train as it passed by. We realized that it was carrying Jews like cattle in the cars. Week after week the whistle would blow. We dreaded to hear the sound of those wheels because we knew that we would hear the cries of the Jews en route to a death camp. Their screams tormented us. We knew the time the train was coming, and when we heard the whistle blow, we began singing hymns. By the time the train came past our church, we were singing at the top of our voices. If we heard the screams, we sang more loudly and soon we heard them no more.

The eyewitness also shared with Lutzer, "Although years have passed, I still hear the train whistle in my sleep. God forgive me, forgive all of us who called ourselves Christians and yet did nothing to intervene."[3]

It's hard to comprehend how they continued living comfortable lives while others were ripped from any normal existence and sent to a hell on earth, tortured, tormented, and killed for no reason other than their nationality, their genes, their associations.

What would I have done? I wondered. *Would I have summoned the courage to stand up against the Nazis? Would I have risked my life to save others?*

I experienced my *Schindler's List* moment when I sat with Sonia, Maria, Nadia, and eleven other women rescued from human trafficking in Greece. But two years before that moment, I experienced something similar, something akin to an awakening, in Auschwitz. I felt a powerful and unshakable conviction that I could no longer sit on the sidelines of humanity's sufferings, of humanity's injustices. Never again could I ignore all those who cry out in pain and terror every day around the globe. Would I be able to persevere even unto death, as Bonhoeffer had? I did not know. All I knew was that I could no longer turn my back on anyone. I had to stand up and be counted. I wasn't around during WWII, but seventy years later, I could do what was needed in my generation.

I looked to heaven and whispered a prayer. "God, help me not to close my eyes to other people's horror or ignore injustice. Help me fight the injustice you hate. Help me value people and speak up for those who have been silenced. God, you have loved, chosen, and healed me, and I want to help set others free. If anything—anything!—like this happens in my lifetime, help me not to sit back and pretend it does not concern me."

God was listening, because in the months to come, he began to awaken me to modern-day atrocities I had no idea were taking place.

My friend and I left Auschwitz that day with heavy hearts. Haunted by the horrors of the camp, I would never be the same. It was as if God had nudged me to wake up from sleepwalking through life, to open my eyes to the living nightmare of others. To awaken to more of the calling he had planned for me.

THERE WAS MORE

I have always been passionate about my work as an evangelist. I've been telling others about the love of Christ since I first started volunteering at my church, setting out chairs for the youth on Wednesday nights, and I've never stopped. I was just twenty-two back then and eager to share the good news in any way I could.

To this day, I love speaking and teaching, bringing the gospel of Christ to people. But that day, as we drove away from Auschwitz, back through those scenic villages, while I couldn't exactly put my finger on it, I knew there was more. I felt that God was drawing me deeper still, stirring something within me that I had intuitively known but never understood. Perhaps something else I was born to do.

I had always envisioned those who fought for justice as the heroes written about in books—other people in other countries, living in different days. Though I'd studied the Holocaust, it seemed distant in time and place. Other atrocities did too: The Cambodian genocide in 1975, during which almost two million people died through political executions, starvation, and forced labor. The Rwandan genocide in 1994, during which an estimated eight hundred thousand people were murdered in just one hundred days. The Bosnian genocide of 1995. Darfur in 2003.

Every documented heinous crime that humanity committed against humanity seemed like history until that day. After Auschwitz, something changed. I grew in an awareness of how we need to fight for justice. I felt energized to rise to what God was calling me to do. Though I wasn't sure what it was specifically.

As I read the words of Jesus, they gripped me like never before. "The Spirit of the Lord is on me, because he has anointed me to preach good news to the poor. He has sent me to proclaim freedom for the prisoners and recovery of sight for the blind, to set the oppressed free."[4] His words kept resounding in my heart. As though they were becoming my own words. The Spirit of the Lord was on *me*. He had anointed *me*. I sensed that something new would be required of me. Of me, not someone else. Often, I had included this very Scripture in my teaching, using it to encourage believers to embrace our corporate responsibility as the church to set people free. But after my visit to Auschwitz, something internally shifted the emphasis from we to me. God was stirring my heart with a direction. *This new love and this new sense of purpose*

*I've put within you are for a reason. Rise up. Get ready. I have more
for you to do.*

God wanted me to rise, ready myself to go, knowing Jesus had
gone on my behalf. I was to go out of love, walking wide awake
through this world, seeing one prisoner yearning to be free, and
then another, and another. God did not want me staying in bed,
resting while a battle raged around me, fought by others. He wanted
me to go, and he wanted me to go with undaunted faith. There
are so many daunting things in the world that we must overcome:
daunting needs, daunting enemies, daunting obstacles. Only the
undaunted—the undaunted in Christ, living in undaunted faith—
will be able to triumph over them. That's what God had been
growing in me. That's why he had set me free, leading me out of
a small, caged existence into a wide-open, spacious life. Mentally.
Emotionally. Spiritually. Physically. In every way. He wanted me to
step into more of the future he had planned for me, so others could
step into more of the future he had planned for them. He wants to
do the same for you.

WAKE UP

My eyes that day were opened to how, by doing nothing when
others suffer, we add to their injury. Once, I saw the persecuted as
in another place, in another time; now I saw myself standing beside
them, willing to fight for them. I realized that the oppressed do not
see much difference between those who keep them down and those
who do nothing to help. For them, there is no in-between.

We who live in privileged conditions don't worry about basic
survival. We don't live in fear for our safety during the simple tasks
of daily life. But this is not the way much of the world lives. The
world in the twenty-first century is not okay. Drought, war, slavery,
drugs, flooding, earthquakes, terrorism, violence, infirmity, lack
of medical help, injustice because of gender or race, embargoes,
disease, debt, famine, unchecked inflation, absence of the rule

of law, refugee status, forced migration—the traumas around the globe are many and varied. Food, water, safety, and protection are just dreams for far too many, the lack of them a daily nightmare. So many people on the earth today spend their days simply trying to stay alive. Trying to survive.

People not unlike you and me, made in God's image, are suffering and trapped all over the world right now. Do you feel disconnected from the people afflicted by these tragedies, just because many of them live in different countries, somewhere "over there," or because you hear about them only on TV or in radio reports? So did I, once, but I've been unable to since that day I walked in the footsteps of the men, women, and children the Germans persecuted and murdered at Auschwitz. How often do you, as I used to, switch channels with your remote when the TV confronts you with some ugly tragedy, or even turn off the television lest you feel some guilt? The people living in those situations can't turn off their pain or the reality of their circumstances like we turn off our TVs.

How could I ever have thought that the world's terror has nothing to do with me? Are these people not loved by God, simply because they live in a different country? Are they not chosen by God, simply because their skin is a different color? Because they speak another language? Could God not lead them out of their caged lives into a wide-open expanse, like he did for me? Do they not matter as much to him as you and I do? Does God not know their name, as he knows ours? Does he not know their pain or their fear? Doesn't God have a destiny in place for each one?

We all know the answer. "Whatever you did for one of the least of these brothers and sisters of mine, you did for me," Jesus said.[5]

If all that I had been teaching about God for years was true, then why couldn't I, wouldn't I, didn't I go and do something? I could not do everything, of course. But I could no longer do nothing. What was I waiting for?

How asleep I had been! How asleep most of us have been! Our disconnection does not make the abuses in this world, the injustices, any less. So many people in the world face oppression in so many different forms. They are trapped by fear, stuck in horrible places, stripped of identity and belonging, disconnected, disenfranchised.

Single moms and single dads are trying to make a family on their own, playing the dual roles of mother and father, serving as nurturer, provider, disciplinarian, taxi driver, home manager, play buddy, spiritual leader, until they are exhausted, worked to death, used up and emotionally wrung out. Absolutely weary.

Many people are alone, having everything they need to live except companionship—isolated, tormented, restless, anxious, hopeless, fearful.

Others wonder how they are going to pay their mortgage or put their kids through school. They wonder if anyone cares if they live or die.

Runaway kids are looking for love and the next meal, a safe place to sleep, ever afraid and ever in pain, desperate.

Addicts are held hostage in a humiliating search for the means to get another fix. They experience emptiness and shame between moments of relief, only to be subject time and time again to horrible twists and turns in body and mind.

I had been asleep. Now God had awakened me so that I could rise ready for what he was calling me to do next.

TIME FOR EYES WIDE OPEN

I felt like the Ephesians when the apostle Paul wrote to them, shaking them out of their slumber. "Wake up, sleeper, rise from the dead, and Christ will shine on you. Be very careful, then, how you live—not as unwise but as wise, making the most of every opportunity, because the days are evil."[6]

When we are asleep, injustice and pain can run rampant across the earth. We may not even see or know of the nightmare someone else is living. But once we've been awakened, we can see the evil and respond. We are up, alert, ready to take the first or next step, ready to make a difference. And yet waking up spiritually is not just about participating in life-changing efforts of worldwide importance, such as stopping genocide. It is walking through our lives wide awake. It is rising ready where we are, being willing to do something with what we have. It is seeing the people around us right where they are and meeting their need.

For some of us, that means being a better spouse and parent, a kinder neighbor, a more engaged church member. It means seeing the world more with God's ever-awake eyes and being Jesus' hands and feet wherever we go. It means looking actively, daily, for practical ways to help people. It means offering grace to the server at the restaurant who forgets to turn in our order, making us wait another fifteen minutes before we get our food.

For each of us, rising ready means seeing our neighbors, understanding the needs right in front of us, and reaching out to meet whatever need presents itself. It means seeing others instead of always looking out for ourselves.

Is there any one of us who can't, in truth, easily forgo two lattes a week in order to sponsor a child through our church's missions program?

Rising ready may mean giving a friend who just lost a job a gift card or buying her lunch, offering to do some shopping for a neighbor trapped at home with a screaming newborn, taking the time to listen to a heartbroken friend whose husband was just diagnosed with cancer. It may mean going through your closet and giving clothes to the local women's shelter.

And for others, like me, it means doing what we can to stop horrific global injustices.

GO FIND SOME DARKNESS

Every day, there are situations in our normal routines that require us to be the light of Christ in the midst of utter darkness. Every day, there are people crossing our paths who need to hear a word of hope, feel a touch of compassion, see the possibility of a different future. We need not look far to find people who need the light of Christ. We need only to be available, looking, willing and obedient to go where they are.

This was made so real to me by something my daughter Sophia once said. It was when we ran a quick errand to the store—a simple errand—that ended with God leaving an indelible mark on my heart.

Nick and I had raced through the aisles, pulling Sophia along with us, and as we were making our way to the checkout, maneuvering to the front of the store, we passed a huge four-sided display of flashlights. Sophia was with us, and at the time, she was obsessed with flashlights—industrial ones, Barbie ones, little ones, big ones, any kind of flashlight. She carried them in her purse, in her backpack, even hid them in her bed under her pillow. She loved the different patterns each one made on her bedroom ceiling long after she was tucked in for the night.

Looking through all the different flashlights, Sophia picked out the one she thought would work best, the one she seemed to think was different from all the others she already possessed, and she flipped on the switch. Staring into the light, even cupping our hands around it, we strained to see as best we could, but none of us could see even a little glow. The giant fluorescent lights of the store were too bright, and the flashlight's meager light was swallowed up.

"Oh, Mummy," Sophia pleaded, "can we please go find some darkness?"

Can we please go find some darkness? From the mouth of babes comes the wisdom of Christ. I couldn't help but be arrested by her innocent question. Darkness is everywhere. We live in a world full of fear and in desperate need of light.

No one could doubt it who had stood, as I had, in Auschwitz, contemplating the unspeakable horrors that had been committed there. Darkness and the fear it carries is everywhere.

But Jesus said, "You are the light of the world. A town built on a hill cannot be hidden. Neither do people light a lamp and put it under a bowl. Instead they put it on its stand, and it gives light to everyone in the house. In the same way, let your light shine before others, that they may see your good deeds and glorify your Father in heaven."[7]

The light overtakes the darkness and the fear. It makes it all disappear. It eradicates its power. It eliminates its strength. Just as sure as morning follows night, the light of Christ is always coming—through us. As his hands and feet, we are the force that conquers the darkness. We. The undaunted ones.

The prophet Isaiah said, "Arise, shine; for your light has come! And the glory of the LORD is risen upon you. For behold, the darkness shall cover the earth, and deep darkness the people; but the LORD will arise over you, and His glory will be seen upon you."[8]

God's glory is upon us, and his light can break through the darkest night. That's why he wants us to partner with him in bringing light into the dark places where oppressors try their best to shut people away.

I understand that we can get worn down by the needs in this world and wearied by them. We need sleep, rest, restoration, recuperation. That's why God gives us the end of a day, and he doesn't begrudge us our rest. He doesn't want us to come to the end of ourselves and be defeated and enslaved in a spiritual Auschwitz, tormented, thinking it is the work we do that sets us free, so that we have to get back up on the treadmill and do more, be more. He doesn't want us to burn the candle at both ends so that we end up lethargic, fatigued, burned up, and burnt out. To do that would be to walk into the lie that was wrought in iron over the arched entrance of Auschwitz. Isn't this is what God meant when he asked in Isaiah 1:12, "Why this frenzy of sacrifices?"[9]

Working ourselves into a frenzy or tormenting others by working them to death is not freedom. It is enslavement.

But we are not slaves. We are free. And we have been freed for a purpose: to share what we've been given. The Bible tells us,

"He has shown you, O man, what is good; and what does the LORD require of you but to do justly, to love mercy, and to walk humbly with your God?"[10]

We do justly and love mercy and walk humbly with our God when we rise ready, when we get up and go out with God to partner with him in his purposes on the earth. Some days, that may mean nothing more than doing a dozen little things throughout your waking hours to love well your family, friends, coworkers, neighbors, and those whose path you cross: listening, running an errand, praying, opening your home, preparing a meal.

And some days, it may mean an assignment much bigger, even dangerous. Flying home from Auschwitz, I knew God was stirring something big in me. He wanted people rescued and restored. That I knew. But who? Reflecting on the camp where millions of Jews were murdered, I thought of King Xerxes in the Bible, who was persuaded by an adviser to issue an edict condemning all the nation's Jews to death. Esther, a Jew but chosen by King Xerxes as his queen, seemed uniquely positioned to persuade the king to withdraw the edict and was urged to do so by her cousin Mordecai, who said, "Who knows but that you have come to your royal position for such a time as this?"[11]

I felt much the same. Who could say that I had not been born into a reasonably affluent and free society for such a time as this? For a time when I could see the injustice and crying need so common throughout the world and stand up to combat it?

Won't you join me? At the very least, pursue what God is calling you to do? You and I have opportunities every day to combat the darkness, the evil, that surrounds us in every country, every corner of the world. The opportunities are countless, and the needs are desperate.

My *Schindler's List* moment lit a fire in me. Let it ignite a similar fire in you. That day I stood in Auschwitz, God reminded me that as hard as it may be to believe, the crimes against his creation, against humanity, are no less egregious today than during the days the ovens were burning at Auschwitz, and those who perpetrate them no less cruel. Genocide, slavery, murder, rape, exploitation— those things exist throughout the world, not just in concentration camps. And they exist now, not just in history.

Whoever saves one life saves the world entire. I will never be able to forget this saying from the Talmud. I don't want to.

Whatever God has called you to do where you are, in your realm of influence, you cannot deny that the darkness that surrounds us is growing. Remember, *you* are the light called to combat that darkness. Together, with God's help, let's defeat the darkness, if even for just one life. And then let's do it for one more, and one more.

Chapter 10

HER NAME
WAS SOPHIA

Fall 2007

Standing in front of the baggage carousel in the Thessaloniki airport in Greece, I waited for my luggage to appear. Having traveled for the last thirty-three hours—from Australia via Singapore and London—I was exhausted. Not having mastered the art of sleeping in an upright position with a screaming child as background music, I hadn't even caught a restful nap. All I wanted to do now was grab my bags and head off to the hotel for a shower, a meal, and some desperately needed sleep.

But the carousel just kept going round and round, with not even one suitcase coming up the ramp. *What's the holdup?* I wondered. *Where are our bags?* I looked around at my fellow bleary-eyed travelers, though there weren't too many at this hour of the night, as our flight had been the last to arrive. Some of them were starting to shuffle restlessly—like me—while others were walking toward the service counters. They too had begun to wonder where our bags were.

As I tried to listen in on their conversations and ascertain whether there was a genuine problem, my stomach grumbled, reminding me that I hadn't eaten in several hours.

"Ladies and gentlemen," a voice began in Greek, making it one of those times I was grateful that, as a child, I'd spoken Greek before I had spoken English, "there is a malfunction with the conveyor equipment that unloads your luggage from the airplane. We're working to repair it as quickly as possible. In the meantime, we are removing your luggage manually. It will take at least another half hour before we can get your bags to the carousel. Thank you for your patience."

Groans resounded all around, and I couldn't blame any of my fellow travelers for their frustration. I was tired too. *But,* I reminded myself, *I am in Greece!* This visit was a dream come true. For almost twenty years, I had been praying for the right opportunity to work with the church here, and being invited to speak at a women's conference was an opened door.

I had always had a deep love and passion for Greece, one that even exceeded my love of feta cheese and olives. I loved the stories my parents told of our Greek heritage. I cherished that even though I was adopted, I was still Greek! After hopping on and off four planes and traversing four airports, I was on the verge of doing something I'd worked toward and dreamed about for so long. *What's another half hour?* I thought. *I'm here!*

The people around me didn't share my enthusiasm and weren't quite so congenial. Some passengers drifted away from the carousel, grumbling, probably in search of coffee or a restaurant, though at this hour nothing was open. Others retired to the corners of the area, some sliding down the walls and sitting on the floor, resigned to the inconvenience. Still others struck up conversations to pass the time.

Tired of sitting the last thirty-three hours and desperate to stretch my legs, I wasn't up for conversation, so I decided to take a walk around the small baggage claim area. Taking in the paint peeling off the walls and the corners scuffed from being sideswiped by too many suitcases and luggage carts, I couldn't help but think the airport seriously needed renovation. Everything seemed so old. Stale. In dire need of updating. *It's little wonder,* I thought, *that the baggage removal equipment has broken down. I don't think they've done anything to keep up the place since the apostle Paul landed by boat.* I chuckled at my own joke, the first smile I'd cracked since landing. It was good to know I could always entertain myself, even as tired as I was.

Taking in more of the neglected airport, I noticed a series of posters plastered along the length of one wall, each featuring the photo of a little girl or a young woman. Each bearing one word stamped in capital letters across the top and bottom: "Missing."

How does someone go missing? I instantly recognized the girl in the picture that was at the center of them all. It was the wide-eyed, sweet face of three-year-old Madeleine McCann. She was the precious little girl discovered missing from her bed six months earlier in Portugal, whose disappearance the international media had been covering nonstop. How could her face not be the most recognizable in the world at that time?[1]

My heart wrenched. Madeleine was between the ages of my firstborn, who was five, and my baby, just fourteen months old. Checking my watch, I calculated it would be early morning at home. They would be just waking up. *Oh, God,* I prayed, *keep them safe. Protect our home.*

I looked back at Madeleine's picture, thinking of the horror her parents must have experienced. They had tucked her into bed, only to go back and check on her and find her missing, no longer lying where she had fallen into an innocent sleep. The word *missing* above and below her photo gripped my heart tighter. Standing there, wondering where on earth she could be, I prayed for her before moving to the next poster—another little girl. And then another. Each depicted just a face, framed like a window that gave me a glimpse of who they were.

Serene. Full of life. Graceful. Playful. Curious.

Their eyes seemed to stare back at me, begging something from me.

As I imagined them, hopefully, alive and waiting to be found, I felt compelled to pray for each one. I called them by name as I prayed. Maria. Anna. Sophia. I gasped. Sophia is my youngest daughter's name. I would never be able to bear the word *missing* on a picture of her. No. Never.

Sophia. I felt a shift inside me. A start. A stop. Something.

The posters seemed to go on forever. Still reading, still praying, I noticed that every missing person had been assigned a case number and a police contact. There were instructions on what to do if you spotted the girl in the photo. But there was no other information. Not whether this little girl loved dolls or that young woman sang beautifully. Whether this one fidgeted or that one loved to twirl round and round.

How much these posters don't say, I thought. *And what does missing mean, anyway? Was this girl abducted, as is suspected in Madeleine's case? Was she taken and murdered?* I shuddered and tried to shake off such an idea. *Did that one run away? Had a natural disaster buried some of these children under rubble? Was this one taken hostage?*

For more than thirty minutes, I moved from poster to poster, studying their faces, wondering how I would feel if one of my daughters went missing. It was a thought I could not bear. I desperately wanted to wrap my arms around my girls and hold them close. *These photographs should be in beautiful frames on a mantel or in the pages of a family photo album on a coffee table,* I thought. *They shouldn't be plastered coldly here, taped across the peeling paint of an airport wall.*

Suddenly my thoughts were interrupted by the boom and rumble of the baggage carousel chugging to life.

"Finally!" several passengers exclaimed.

Turning toward the baggage claim area, I slowly made my way back there, still trying to comprehend how so many women and children could be missing. *How could this be possible? Why isn't more being done about this?* Not feeling quite as assertive as my fellow passengers, I waited behind them. As they claimed their bags, one by one, and the crowd thinned, I peered between them for my bags. Just when I started to grow concerned that they hadn't made my last connecting flight, there they were.

MISSING SOMETHING

Stepping outside, taking in a breath of fresh air, I spotted the pastors who were hosting me and the conference. They were just pulling up to the curb. Jumping out of the car and rushing to grab my bags, they apologized for their delay, having no idea they were right on time. It was my bags that had been late. After I explained, they assured me that they would soon give me a feast that would make me forget all the inconvenience. Being hospitable hosts, and true to Greek form, they thought a meal would be the quickest remedy for baggage delays, jet lag, or anything else that ailed me. I already felt so at home!

We drove to a restaurant where several leaders from their church were waiting to welcome us with great fellowship and lots of food. Seeing the vast spread on the table, I smiled to myself. *Of course we will be eating dinner until midnight. I am in Greece!*

Although I was incredibly grateful, I was deliriously tired, and I didn't want to offend my hosts. I had always respected the customs of people in any country I visited—and their hospitality—so I decided I would just have to find my second, third, or fourth wind.

Over dinner, we chatted about the state of the church in Greece, and my new friends shared how they hoped this conference would be a defining moment for the women of their city. But as we discussed details about the week ahead, I found myself mentally drifting back to those posters at the airport. The faces of those children and young women wouldn't stop taunting the corners of my mind. I picked up my coffee cup and rested its hot lip against my cheek for a moment. Finally, I could stand it no longer. I had to ask the question that had been burning inside me for more than an hour.

"Have you seen all those posters of missing people at the airport?" I asked.

"Yes," my host answered, and everyone else nodded.

"Why are there so many missing children and young women?"

"Mmm," my host responded, quickly swallowing a bite. "It's suspected that they were kidnapped, which seems to happen frequently these days. It's so tragic." She paused. "We don't know what else we can do other than pray for them."

A few seconds of quiet followed her comment, and then the conversation drifted back to the conference. I politely joined in but could not shake all those innocent faces from the posters. I had come to minister to the women of Greece who would attend this conference, and I was excited about that, but my heart had now been stirred, and my thoughts were consumed by the faces of the missing.

IT'S NOT BUSINESS—IT'S PERSONAL

A few hours later, in the dark hours of the morning, I suddenly jolted awake. Dazed. Shaken. Disoriented. I blinked open my eyes, trying to remember where I was. It took me a minute, but then it came to me. *The hotel room. Yes. Thessaloniki.* Looking at the sheets twisted about me, I realized it was my own tossing and turning that had roused me. I fluffed my pillow and turned over to try to fall asleep again.

Instead the faces from the posters danced across my mind, waking me further. Sighing in surrender, I knew there would be no more sleep tonight. I sat up and threw back the covers. Somewhere inside, I knew God wanted my attention.

I began to think about my message, the one I would teach in a few hours. It was about the parable of the good Samaritan, the story Jesus told. I knew the passage by heart. I'd read and heard the story many times and had reviewed and studied it repeatedly in recent months, specifically for this conference. It seemed to burn in me, now more than ever. Turning on the lamp, I reached for my Bible and began to read. "A certain man went down from Jerusalem to Jericho, and fell among thieves, who stripped him of his clothing, wounded him, and departed, leaving him half dead."[2]

I thought of the many people in modern times who are in situations just like this man was. Hurt and wounded, they are lying on the side of so many roads, left behind by abuse, addiction, imprisonment, loss, famine, disease, violence, tyranny, and oppression. People broken by injustice, stripped of their belongings, dignity, identity, and self-worth. I kept reading. "Now by chance a certain priest came down that road. And when he saw him, he passed by on the other side. Likewise a Levite, when he arrived at the place, came and looked, and passed by on the other side. But a certain Samaritan, as he journeyed, came where he was. And when he saw him, he had compassion. So he went to him and bandaged his wounds, pouring on oil and wine; and he set him on his own animal, brought him to an inn, and took care of him."[3]

He went to him? For some reason, as many times as I'd heard this story, those words had never registered like they did now. I went back over that phrase. *So he went to him. So he went to him.*

Like a song stuck in my head, the phrase replayed in my mind over and over.

At first, I couldn't understand why those five words jumped out at me with such force. Defensively, I asked, "Lord, don't I spend my life going to broken people? After all, haven't I just traveled more than thirty-three hours across the globe to come and speak life, hope, and liberty to those who are spiritually and emotionally bound and hopeless? What are you saying to me?"

I felt such an urging to read the passage once more, this time more slowly. Moving through it, reading it carefully, I felt as if I'd been blind the many times I'd read it before, but now I could see. It was as though I could feel scales falling from my eyes.

Before, when I read the story, I had always thought of myself as the good Samaritan. After all, I was an itinerant evangelist who spent most of the year on the road, making it my business to go to *them*—the broken and those dying in ditches, perhaps in ditches of their own making, perhaps thrown there by the cruelty of others. I had a well-thought-out schedule, carefully planned so I could reach as many people as possible. Now I was reading between the lines of Jesus' story, and I was beginning to understand. *But what about those you did not plan to go to, those you have been walking past for years on the way to those you chose to reach? What about the young women and children on the posters at the airport? The ones you've never considered, the ones you never knew existed?*

Nowhere in Jesus' story does it say that the priest or the Levite were bad people. But they were busy people, religious people. They were so consumed with keeping their schedules, appointments, and commitments that they ended up walking past someone they should have helped. The man lying on the side of the road was an interruption to their ministry rather than a reason for it.

Oh, Lord, I asked, *how have I never seen such posters before? I travel through so many airports around the world. Have I just walked by and not seen?*

Yes. I realized I had looked at them in the airport in Kiev, but what I was looking at never really registered in my mind. I had looked but not seen.

How often do we miss what is right under our noses because we're looking but we're not seeing?

Gripping my chest as though I could really steady my heart, I kept asking God questions. *Am I really any different from the priest who, on his way to some priestly duty, saw the man lying wounded and broken and simply passed by on the other side? Am I any different from the Levite who looked, saw, and then went on his way?*

My desperate pleas began to give way to understanding. The only difference between the Samaritan and the religious people was that the Samaritan crossed the street. The Samaritan was willing to interrupt his plans so he could assist the man. The Samaritan stopped and stooped down to lift up the broken one. Stopping and stooping are the responses God wants from us. Compassion is what God desires, but compassion is only emotion until you cross the street. Until you stop and stoop. Compassion means responding. Taking action. Going to the lost of the world. The missing.

I wanted to weep.

I saw in my mind Jesus, who not only crossed the road from heaven to earth but also stopped to see our hurts and heal our wounds. He looked at us, and then he stooped to bear the cross for us, carrying it to the hill where he was nailed to it in our stead.

CALLED TO STOP AND STOOP

During my visit to Auschwitz, I had been jarred awake by the appalling evidence of people's inhumanity to other people. I had cringed and shuddered in a flood of empathy for those who had suffered unspeakable acts in that place. And although I had not fully understood on that day what God was doing in me, I saw clearly and powerfully for the first time a multitude of needs around the world, needs related to injustice, poverty, oppression, war, and disaster.

Now God was taking me to the next step. He was reaching into my life, not just to make me aware but to stop me and turn my steps toward those in need so that, like the Samaritan, I could stoop to help them. I was realizing the difference in responses, that it is one thing to be awakened to injustice and quite another to be willing to be interrupted and inconvenienced to do something about it.

I had stared into the faces on those posters in the airport. I had prayed for them. But now there was a question in my heart begging for an answer. How could I turn and walk away from the oppressed and wounded once I had stared into their eyes and felt them stare back at me?

I couldn't. Not that night, sitting in my hotel room, my Bible on my lap, the story of the good Samaritan in my head, the image in my heart of Jesus struggling up the road to the cross. And I couldn't the next week, either, when I got back on a plane to fly home.

The faces on those posters in the airport imprinted themselves on my mind and followed me all the way home.

I knew that I could not go on with ministry as usual. I knew I had to follow in the footsteps of the Samaritan, of Jesus. I had to reach out to the missing. Though I had no idea how or when and with what.

For months thereafter, I searched for answers. I made phone calls. I asked questions. I scoured the internet. I visited agencies. I discovered that the faces I'd seen on those posters were not just randomly missing people or runaways. They were, allegedly, victims of human trafficking.

I didn't even know what human trafficking meant until someone explained to me it was slavery.

Slavery, I argued, had been abolished. The world knew about President Abraham Lincoln and the Emancipation Proclamation of 1863 and the Thirteenth Amendment of 1865. Everyone knew about the laws banning serfdom and the domino effect that began around the world in the 1800s as a result of Lincoln's courage. Virtually every nation had passed laws banning slavery. More than a century later, how could there possibly still be slavery?

There was much for me to learn. Everything about the recruiting, transporting, and harboring of people for the purpose of exploitation, whether they were to be used for forced labor, domestic servitude, or sex. I came to realize that slavery had not been abolished. Not at all.

It just had a new name. With a modern twist. Hidden in plain sight. Often, run by organized crime. A global pandemic.

Human trafficking. The very term sounded so inhumane. So desensitizing. So shattering. Much like numbers assigned to people in a concentration camp. Millions were murdered then. In plain sight. Now millions more were being trafficked. In plain sight.

As I continued to study, to research, to educate myself, I learned there are tens of millions of people being lured, kidnapped, taken as slaves in our lifetime, on our watch. Not in some other time.

Not in history. But right now. Today. While we're going about our daily routines, getting kids ready in the morning, hopping in the car to drop them off at school and head on to work. While we're eating dinner, while we're winding down and sleeping through the night.

Tens of millions of people like you and me, with faces and families, are being bought and sold like goods and commodities, with no choice, no rights. Traded for money. In Eastern European countries. In Southeast Asia. In Western Europe. In the Middle East. In South America. In the United States. Right where we live.

How can I possibly reach them all? It was a question I asked the Lord over and over again.

Then one day, as I was praying, I had a moment. *How can I be sure, Lord, that you're leading me to this deep, dark ditch where awaits not one victim but tens of millions of them? How can I free them all?*

No sooner had I formed that thought than I had to laugh at myself. After all, wasn't I acquainted with what numbers could do? Wasn't I number 2508? Hadn't someone crossed the street to see me and help me? Hadn't someone heard my cry, felt my pain, and chosen not to walk on by but to lift me out of my brokenness into the loving arms of Jesus? My parents had adopted me. Loved me. Raised me. Someone told me about Jesus. Someone invited me to church. Someone encouraged me to grow, to lead, to speak.

What right did I have to be overwhelmed by numbers?

I sensed God urging me on. *Stop. Stoop. You have already helped so many in all the ditches I've sent you to. Now cross the street to these.*

How different a divine interruption is from an awakening. God had gently led me to an awakening at Auschwitz. He was preparing me then for what he was calling me to do now. Nine months before my trip to Thessaloniki, he was already at work, readying my heart, readying me to step into more of my calling. Preparing me for even more good works.

He was showing me that the Samaritan not only went to the broken one but did more: the Samaritan gave the man in the ditch medical supplies and transportation, and the Samaritan paid for the man's restoration. The Samaritan, the true neighbor, is the one who gives not only his time but also his talent and treasure. He goes the full distance.

The more I understood what God was calling me to do, the more undaunted I grew. I wanted to do this. I wanted to do for others what had been done for me. It was just as Joseph said to his brothers in the book of Genesis: "You intended to harm me, but God intended it for good to accomplish what is now being done, the saving of many lives."[4]

I, who had been rescued from a hospital where I was left unwanted and unnamed, could help rescue others from the same kind of hopelessness. I could help them be valued, loved, and restored. I could help orchestrate a future for them.

No sooner had I felt so inspired to stop and stoop then I immediately began to think of one hundred reasons not to, one hundred reasons to feel daunted.

Isn't that how we all are? We're roused to do something, and then we immediately forget the one reason why we are capable of doing anything at all. When I discovered the magnitude of the problem of human trafficking, I was so overwhelmed that I began to compile a list of all the reasons why a forty-year-old mother of two living on the other side of the world could not possibly do anything that would significantly change the statistics. And my list sounded just like everyone else's.

- But God, I don't know enough about the issue.
- But God, I'm not educated enough to get involved.
- But God, I'm not skilled enough.
- But God, I already have enough on my plate.
- But God, I have a family.
- But God, it's too dangerous.
- But God, I'm too old to start something new.
- But God, I'm too young to be taken seriously.
- But God, this will tip the scales of balance in my life.

And on the list goes. Maybe a list like this is what kept the priest going on his way. *But I'm not a doctor. I can't help. That man's brokenness is bigger than I know how to tend. I should go on to those I do know how to help.*

Maybe the Levite, who came closer, thought something similar. *This is way too big for me. I'm not strong enough to lift this fellow. I can't carry him. I don't belong in this world. I need to stay focused on what I already know God wants me to do.*

Why do we disqualify ourselves before we ever even get started? It's time we understand that God doesn't call the qualified. He qualifies the called.

The apostle Paul wrote this to the Corinthians—and to us: "Not that we are sufficiently qualified in ourselves to claim anything as coming from us, but our sufficiency and qualifications come from God. He has qualified us."[5]

We have to believe that God has called us to go into the world in his name, and not listen to the paralyzing labels and limitations imposed on us by ourselves, others, or our enemy. We cannot allow them to daunt us. Whom God calls, he qualifies, and he chooses everybody to do something specific, something that is part of his design. The Bible shows us that since the beginning of time, God has chosen the unlikely to do the unimaginable.

• *God called Moses* to confront Pharaoh when Moses was eighty years old. Initially, Moses insisted that he was not eloquent and that no one would listen to him. But God lifted Moses' eyes off Moses and up to him: "Who makes a person's mouth? Who decides whether people speak or do not speak, hear or do not hear, see or do not see? Is it not I, the LORD? Now go! I will be with you as you speak, and I will instruct you in what to say."[6] When Moses finally stopped making excuses and did as God told him to, God paved a way for him—right through the middle of the Red Sea and across the desert, all the way to the entrance of the promised land.

- *God called Gideon* a "mighty warrior,"[7] telling Gideon to save his people, who were being relentlessly ransacked by their enemies. At the time, Gideon was working in a hidden place because he feared the enemy. He couldn't imagine how God could use a coward to fight for his people. "I'm from the weakest of your tribes," he protested, but God promised, "I'll be strong where you are weak."[8] And he was, enabling Gideon, with just three hundred soldiers, to defeat the enemy's army of a million.

- *God called Jeremiah,* a teenager, to deliver news to the Jewish people, but Jeremiah feared that as young as he was, he wouldn't be taken seriously. God said, "Before you were born I set you apart."[9] So for twenty-four years Jeremiah did all God asked, writing two books filled with God's words. Though the first book was destroyed and Jeremiah was imprisoned, God sent rescuers and made a way for his message to be delivered.

That's how God works. I have no doubt that nearly every person who reads this book has been called by God for a task outside his or her comfort zone, maybe way outside it. How easy it would be to respond like Moses, Gideon, or Jeremiah.

- "Lord, I have no experience."
- "I'm not tech savvy enough."
- "I don't really have the right education."
- "I'm too old [or too young]."
- "I don't know the right people."
- "I'm not smart [or hip or cool or brave] enough."
- "I have no idea where to start."

Moses, Gideon, and Jeremiah would have missed out on their moment in history if they'd been allowed to get by with those kinds of excuses. We wouldn't even know their names today. We know who they were because God refused to accept their excuses.

God insisted they accept his assignment, and then he provided them with everything they needed to succeed in it.

Isn't that what he's done for us?

The more we know him, the more we fulfill our calling and walk into our future with him, the more undaunted we will live, and the more prepared we will be for fulfilling even more assignments he's called us to do. That's what a life of faith is—taking risks and trusting God. It's progressing through levels of trust, giving God more and more of our hearts with each step forward.

What is God calling you to do? Who is God calling you to reach?

Maybe you see a rise in teen pregnancy in your community, but you're a mom of elementary-aged daughters. How easy it would be to think, *What do I know about teenagers anyway? Why would they listen to me? How could I ever help them when I can't even keep up with my own life, let alone find homes or resources for teen moms and their babies?*

Maybe you see a TV commercial highlighting the plight of starving children in Africa and wonder, *What difference could I possibly make on the other side of the world? I'm just trying to keep my own kids on track!*

How easy it is to let the depth of a ditch or the severity of someone's brokenness stop a good work before we stoop down to it. How often we pray for God to use us for his purpose, and then when he interrupts our lives to answer our prayer, we list all our inadequacies. Our objections. Our fears.

When I protested, *How can I alone reach tens of millions of people?* God kept asking, *Will you cross the street and reach out to one?*

He never asks us to cross the street because we have the capacity, in and of ourselves, to rescue hurting people. He asks because he has it.

NO GIFT TOO SMALL

When God invites us to cross the street, he never asks us to go alone. He goes along. He goes ahead. He's by our side. He never leaves us nor forsakes us.[10] He's within us, doing the work through us.[11]

This means that while we may think we don't have enough time, money, resources, or know-how for the task, God will use what we have.

He doesn't ask, "Are you capable?"

He asks, "Are you willing?"

And he does the rest. It's important to remember this, because otherwise we may be so convinced that our contribution will be so small, so insignificant, so inconsequential that we decide to do nothing.

Jesus has always used small things to make a big difference. In John 6, he used a young boy's lunch to feed five thousand people. I'm sure that if you'd asked the boy that morning if he had brought enough food to feed the whole crowd, he'd have laughed. "With five little loaves of bread and two fishes? There are thousands of people here! We'd be lucky to each get a piece the size of a pebble." If you had asked him what he was doing, then, offering his lunch to Jesus, he might well have said, "He might be hungry, and even though I don't have enough lunch for everyone, I have enough for one person. I'll let him eat my lunch."

But once he'd given that small gift to Jesus, Jesus used it to do something far beyond what that boy imagined or expected. So it is with our small gifts in his hands.

Whatever we receive from God is what he asks us to give to someone else. This is exactly what Jesus meant when he said, "Freely you have received; freely give."[12]

I saw the power of this the time my own Sophia and I were walking down a crowded street. I had a full day but had promised to let her accompany me—a special treat for both of us. I was racing the clock, determined to make it to Starbucks before a meeting. We'd been running hard and fast all that day to keep appointments, to get things done, and I needed a pick-me-up. Images of grande cups full of nonfat cappuccinos, extra, extra, extra dry, extra, extra hot, with extra foam, were dancing in my head.

Sophia, on the other hand, would have been happy just to

meander along and look at everything: the window displays, the giant pots filled with trees and flowers outside of buildings, even the cars parked alongside the curb. But I was on a mission.

Suddenly I realized that Sophia's hand was no longer in mine. I grabbed at the air, reaching for her, but touched nothing. Whirling around to find her, I spied her just steps behind. She had stopped to kneel at the curb next to a man who appeared to be destitute. She was holding out to him a dollar I'd given her that morning to buy a treat for herself—a dollar she had cherished the entire day. It was a treasure, a rare gift for a special day with Mummy, and she'd been trying to decide exactly how to spend it on our day downtown. Now, without hesitation, she was freely handing it to a complete stranger.

"Jesus gave me this dollar to give to you," I heard her saying.

I marveled at how easily she was handing over what was so precious to her. How powerful that mere dollar had become.

The man she handed it to handed it back, tears streaming down his face. "Honey," he said, "you spend that on some candy for yourself."

He had been given something far more precious than her dollar. Sophia had extended to him her heart—and so much more. She had given him hope. She had reminded him that there was goodness in this world, and grace, even from a child. She had reminded him that God would provide, even from the least and most unlikely sources. Sophia had crossed the street—or at least moved to the side of it—and God had gone with her. He used her open hand to open a stranger's heart. And he used her willing spirit that day to show me that when we give what we have, and don't overthink it, then God—the God of hope—delivers all the rest.

Chapter 11

NOTHING
IS IMPOSSIBLE

Wait, Nick," I said, pressing the phone closer to my ear, "they're making an announcement. I can't hear you. Hold on." Still standing in the middle of the terminal, I lowered my phone and opened my purse wide. Reaching across the counter, I raked all the contents back into my purse, from which I'd dumped them out in a frantic search for my phone. I had been determined not to miss Nick's call. I could feel fellow passengers brushing past me, maneuvering around me. Glancing up apologetically, I couldn't miss the frowns or smirks some threw back at me over their shoulders. I really hadn't intended to be in everyone's way.

Still waiting for the loud and nearly unintelligible announcement to come screeching to a halt, I shook everything to the bottom of my bag and made my way around the counter to the side of the walkway, away from the crowds passing by. Nestling the phone against my ear again, I was eager to hear what Nick had to say.

"Hi, babe. I can hear you now."

Nick had gone ahead of me to Greece and had been there a few days, preparing the way. I was catching a flight to meet him.

"Chris," he began in his serious tone, "we need to talk."

Instantly I was unnerved. Even answering his call had started my heart to pump a little faster, though I always loved talking to Nick about anything. It's just that when I'm traveling, phone calls always startle me. I'm not entirely sure why, but because of the constant travel and unreliable phone coverage, I typically communicate through text and email. So when someone calls, particularly if it's Nick, I brace myself, knowing something's up. I knew that if it weren't urgent, he would have reached out to me in a less direct way. Whatever Nick had called about, I could sense the gravity of it. His somber tone was a real giveaway.

As he started to speak, I couldn't stop the bottom from falling out of my stomach, and I couldn't stop myself from jumping right in. "Are the kids all right? Is it Mum? Has anything happened?" My mind was racing faster than I was talking, thinking of a dozen more possibilities, but Nick interrupted me just in time.

"Yes, no, no," Nick said. "Everyone is fine. I just want to give you a heads-up about the report the consultants are going to present when you arrive, because . . ." He paused. "I know you are not going to like it."

Although I'd long since learned to trust Nick completely, I still didn't like surprises. And something big had to be up for him to feel the need to prepare me like this for the meeting ahead, one scheduled with several consultants we'd hired to help us think through the launch of our next big initiative: a nongovernmental organization (NGO) to combat human trafficking.

After my baggage claim experience in Thessaloniki, when I saw all those posters of the missing—especially the one of the little girl named Sophia—and after about fifteen months of discussions with our senior pastors, extensive prayer, and much soul searching, Nick and I agreed to take a leap of faith. We could not ignore the international crisis of human trafficking. We could not go back to ministry as usual. We decided to take action. We believed God was calling us to start an organization to reach, rescue, and restore the lives of those impacted by human trafficking. We had a multistep vision for eradicating it through prevention, identification, and aftercare, even though we had no idea how to do any of it. We called it The A21 Campaign, as shorthand for "abolishing injustice in the twenty-first century."

That had been only three months ago, and now, all too soon, Nick was telling me I would hear news I wasn't going to like.

"Chris," Nick continued, "after twenty-five days of extensive research, discussions with government authorities, law enforcement, legal representatives, and other NGOs, well, you're not going to believe this. The consultants have come to the conclusion that we should not start our work in Europe with an emphasis on Eastern Europe because—in their words—it's certain to fail. The difficulties ahead are insurmountable."

The conclusion? I wasn't sure I was hearing this right. We'd already known, even before we hired the consultants, that there were many reasons why starting A21 in Greece didn't make sense. We knew the challenges. We had discussed them at great length. And we had decided that we could not ignore God's call, regardless of the difficulty. That decision had already been made. We had hired the consultants to help us navigate the troubled waters we knew lay ahead of us, not to make our decision for us.

With great frustration I continued listening to Nick. "Their research suggests there are too many factors working against us for A21 to have any chance of success in Eastern Europe. There's too much corruption, and there aren't enough laws to protect the rights of victims. The women will be reluctant to testify against their traffickers, since their own well-being and that of all those they love has already been threatened. Search and rescue would be extremely dangerous, because criminal networks have huge strongholds in all areas of society where we would be going. Prostitution is legal there, and awareness of human trafficking is nonexistent, so we'll have a tough time garnering support. And with the state of the economy, our costs for an operation of this magnitude are going to be sky-high. They're not convinced we'll be able to get the financial backing."

Nick was right. I didn't like what I heard, and I couldn't believe I was hearing it. My annoyance only escalated. "You mean after twenty-five days, all we've got is a list of how hard the challenge will be and why this can't work? And that isn't even an original list. We pointed out to them all those same problems at the initial meeting!"

I was stunned.

How can they be so bold as to tell us what we have already told them? We paid good money to qualified consultants so they could help us find a way to succeed, and the only thing they can tell us is that it's impossible?

We had not asked the consultants *if* we could run an anti–human trafficking initiative in Greece. We had asked them *how* to start one. We already knew that the odds were stacked against us. We knew the degree of darkness we would be entering. What we didn't know was where we should begin. That's why we needed their advice. What steps do we take? What should we prepare for and how? Where could we find resources?

As scores of people walked past me in the airport, time seemed to stand still. I began listing in my mind all the things we needed to determine, and as I did, my resolve only strengthened. *Of course this campaign will be difficult. If it were easy, then it would have already been done. Everyone would have already eradicated the problem. There wouldn't be posters of the missing displayed in airports throughout the world. There wouldn't be any victims of human trafficking!*

To these highly experienced consultants, our idea—which we believed was God's idea—looked impossible. And maybe it was. But impossible is where God starts!

I couldn't help but feel like the Israelites in the Old Testament when they faced the Philistine army and its many giants, the most famous being a champion named Goliath. To this day, his name is used for anything of a monstrous size. Just mention the name Goliath, and people know you mean something big. Really big. Goliath was legendary but not invincible.

When he walked the earth, he and his fellow giants towered over the Israelites. They were from the city of Gath, and they were known for their great size. When the Philistines faced the Israelites in battle, it was Goliath who yelled insults from their side, taunting the Israelites and filling them with fear. Day after day, for forty days, he intimidated them, begging for a man to come forward and fight him one on one.[1] A man he thought he would easily defeat. A man whose failure would ensure the domination of the Philistines. "Goliath stood and shouted to the ranks of Israel, 'Why do you come out and line up for battle? Am I not a Philistine, and are you not the servants of Saul? Choose a man and have him come down to me. If he is able to fight and kill me, we will become your subjects; but if I overcome him and kill him, you will become our subjects and serve us.' Then the Philistine said, 'This day I defy the armies of Israel! Give me a man and let us fight each other.'"[2]

Goliath's taunts left the Israelites and King Saul, their leader, "dismayed and terrified."[3] Every time Goliath came out to sling his insults, "they all fled from him in great fear."[4]

It is so easy to flee, to run in fear. Whether we run physically or just withdraw internally, it's so tempting to succumb to the raw power of fear. Too often we shrink our lives, even to the point of denying our calling. Wasn't that the real issue I faced when I found myself desperate to overcome my fear of flying? I was so tempted to pull back, to limit my reach, to compromise my willingness to obey. But there were people—lost people, missing people, hurting people—on the other side of my obedience. Thank God for his words of truth that helped me to press through my fear: "God has not given us a spirit of fear, but of power and of love and of a sound mind."[5]

I hadn't overcome fear then to get to this place now in my journey only to cave. God had called us to start A21. We couldn't shut down or scale back. We couldn't let the words of this Goliath of a report daunt us. We couldn't let them strike fear in our hearts.

We had to act like David when he heard about Goliath. Still

boy, he came to the battlefield to bring his brothers some lunch. Not knowing what all the ruckus was about, he asked some men, "What will be done for the man who kills this Philistine and removes this disgrace from Israel? Who is this uncircumcised Philistine that he should defy the armies of the living God?"[6]

The answer: "The king will give great wealth to the man who kills him. He will also give him his daughter in marriage and will exempt his family from taxes in Israel."[7]

Never give an impetuous teenage boy a challenge like that.

David went to King Saul and said, "Let no one lose heart on account of this Philistine; your servant will go and fight him."[8]

David had no fear. No matter how big the giant was. No matter how intimidating he sounded.

How could Nick and I do any less? There were missing men, women, and children to be found. To be rescued. To be restored. That's what God had called us to do.

David went out to face Goliath. A boy. Armed with a sling and five smooth stones. And the Word of God. "You come against me with sword and spear and javelin, but I come against you in the name of the LORD Almighty, the God of the armies of Israel, whom you have defied. This day the LORD will deliver you into my hands, and I'll strike you down and cut off your head. This very day I will give the carcasses of the Philistine army to the birds and the wild animals, and the whole world will know that there is a God in Israel. All those gathered here will know that it is not by sword or spear that the LORD saves; for the battle is the LORD's, and he will give all of you into our hands."[9]

Like David, Nick and I had the Word of the Lord. Verse after verse that we had been praying, like so many I have shared in this book.

- Greater is he who is in us than he who is in the world.[10]
- What is impossible with man is possible with God.[11]
- If God be for us, who can be against us?[12]

- God is with us. Always. To the end of the age.[13]
- God will never leave us. Never will he forsake us.[14]
- God promises to make a way where there is no way.[15]
- God is pleased when we walk by faith.[16]
- God told us to go into all the world.[17]
- And my favorite that David spoke: The battle is the Lord's.[18]

David knew that whatever happened as he faced the giant Goliath, the God of Israel would be with him and the battle would be the Lord's.

When the time came, David ran quickly toward the battle line to meet Goliath. Reaching in his bag, David pulled out one smooth stone and slung it, striking Goliath. The stone sank into the giant's forehead, and he fell to the ground. David defeated Goliath with a simple sling and one smooth rock.

Backed by the Word of God.

Backed by the will of God.

Backed by what God had called him to do.

How could Nick and I face our giants with any less faith than David's? We couldn't. We knew that the consultants were paid to turn their experience loose on our problems and to offer their honest opinions, positive or negative. But in this case, what we needed was not help in identifying the giants. We already knew there were giants, and we knew where they were. What we needed was help in finding the stones we would use to destroy them.

Finding my resolve, I straightened up my frame to my full five feet and two inches and took a deep breath, just as I imagined David might have done. To the world, A21's mission didn't make sense. But our foundation for believing that it would succeed trumped the world's information. We had chosen to believe God's Word, no matter what.

"Nick," I said loudly, "we need to tell them that God has already given us the victory. Tell them that we are well able to do this because he is with us. Tell them that we know they're right, that this makes no sense in earthly terms. Nevertheless, we will go, because God can make a way where others say there is no way."

I was more convinced than ever that we were on the right track. True, I was no clearer on how we were going to bring about change for those enslaved in human trafficking, but I knew we had to do it.

Thank you, God, I prayed after I said goodbye to Nick. *Thank you for being the God who helps us to overcome challenges and difficult circumstances, for being the God who makes a way where there is no way. Now help us figure out the next step, and the step after that.*

And just as I said amen, another blaring announcement pierced the air. "All passengers on Aegean Airlines flight to Thessaloniki, Greece, we are now boarding. Those on Aegean Airlines to Thessaloniki, Greece, board at gate A21."

DIFFICULT, YES. IMPOSSIBLE, NO.

Gate A21. Sometimes God has to shout over the crowds, over all the noise and clamor in our lives, for us to understand that although there will always be difficulties in this world, the one who created the universe can overcome them all.

This was one of those times.

By choosing, at the exact time A21 was under fire, to have my flight leave from gate A21, God was reminding me of who was in charge. It was as though he was confirming that we were right on course. I knew the facts, Nick knew the facts, and both of us knew the truth.

Yes, the odds were stacked against us. Overwhelmingly.

Yes, every bit of reason and all the advice we'd paid for said to stop before we even started.

Yes, the giants we were facing could make us think there was no way forward.

But none of those things could stop us, not when we were daring to do what God had called us to do. Not when we were pursuing his will.

Would it be difficult? Yes. We had God's Word on that. "In the world you will have tribulation," Jesus promised, and then he added, "but be of good cheer, I have overcome the world."[19]

Would it be impossible? No. We had God's Word on that too. "What is impossible with man is possible with God."[20]

There is nothing he cannot do. Not in my life. And not in yours. God is always with us and always making a way for us to do his will, to bring his hope and change into this world. But so many times in our lives, there's so much temptation to think otherwise, like when

- we're asked to speak to a group but think, *I can't! I'm too shy. I'm not a public speaker.*
- we want to volunteer at a local shelter, but our schedule tells us that we're too busy and cannot add one more thing.
- we want to give some money or groceries and goods to a family burned out of their home, but our checkbook says there's not enough in our account to pay even our own bills, let alone help with someone else's.
- we want to make a career change to follow what we know is our calling, yet our confidence mutters, *Stay where you are. There are too many unknowns! It makes no sense to give up a job other people would give anything to have, just to try for some fleeting sense of happiness.*

Difficulty is the bully that steps into our path and tries to wrestle us to the ground and pin us until we cry uncle. No matter what we're trying to do, if it's worthwhile, he will try to outshout both God and our own thoughts until he confuses us. He will loom so large that we can see only what's right in front of us—the problems, the obstacles, and all the reasons to stop.

Difficulty always sings a dirge of defeat: whatever it is you're trying to do will take too much time, money, risk, strength, willpower—and on and on.

Difficulty loves to sing about hurdles that have been around since the beginning of time. Isn't that what Goliath was really saying to the Israelites? You're too small. Too weak. Too insignificant.

But when God has called you to do something, he will always make a way where there is no way. We just have to remember that difficult isn't impossible. It's just difficult. It's a place we move through on our way to where God wants us to go.

THE POWER OF PRAYER

The greatest giants we face have such common names: Discouragement. Disappointment. Insecurity. Fear. Rejection. Betrayal. Setback. Shortage. Detour. But David knew that the Word of the Lord defeats giants. The name of the Lord defeats giants.[21] And the best way to use the Word of the Lord and the name of the Lord is with the weapon called prayer.[22]

Prayer allows us to knock giants like Difficulty off their feet, because there's power when we pray. "The earnest (heartfelt, continued) prayer of a righteous man makes tremendous power available [dynamic in its working]."[23]

Prayer is a power like no other, a great first option, not just a last resort. When we move into the future praying, faith rises. We grow undaunted, and miracles begin to happen. The impossible becomes possible.

So not knowing what else to do, Nick and I mobilized everyone we knew to pray through every difficulty the consultants told us would make the success of A21 impossible.

Our first prayer assignment was our first challenge—to establish an aftercare home for rescued victims. We'd opened our legal office in Thessaloniki and hired a lawyer and operations manager, but authorities told us it would take at least two years to get all the approvals and permits to open and operate an aftercare home, and there were no guarantees that we would be given the necessary permits once our application had been processed.

There was nothing to do but watch and pray, and as we prayed, our lawyer turned in our applications and met with the regional anti–human trafficking unit. She boldly shared her passion to see girls rescued and restored, and a strange thing happened. She told about one of her own children who had died, and how, although she would never hold him on this earth again, she could help other parents hold their children. "Please," our lawyer pleaded with the authorities, "please help me to help others out of this pain."

The head of the regional office began to weep. In the course of her work, she had never heard such a passionate, sincere, and authentic plea.

That very day, we received the necessary permit. One-day approval never, ever happens in Greece. And this was in December, less than a month after the negative report from the consultants! Not only did we receive the permit, but also we were granted premises—a safe home that was already registered and available. All we had to do was come up with the money to renovate it and pay the rent.

God gave us not only what we needed—the permit—but more: the house.

Not surprisingly, though, Difficulty once again reared its head. We couldn't afford the cost of the monthly rent.

Again we prayed, *Lord, make a way.* Soon we received calls from people at various churches, asking how they could help support this new work. We'd prayed for help, and God didn't just show us where to get help; he brought it to us.

That's how it went with each step we took to build A21. We prayed our way forward through every difficulty—for divine alignments, for favor, for resources, and for open doors. And where the consultants had said there was no way, God made a way. Time and time again. He moved hearts and paperwork and houses and delivered not only what was needed but also so much more.

When the Greek authorities who conducted the investigations into human trafficking were hampered by cuts in funding, we prayed for them too.

We have a safe home, we prayed, *so please, God, bring us the girls who need help.*

Earnestly we prayed, in shifts, around the clock. *God, if you want these girls to find freedom, you'll have to make a way. If the police can't fund investigations, you'll have to convict the clients to help us. Work on their hearts.*

Not long after, a man walked into the police station with a girl who spoke only broken Greek. It turned out she had been a victim of human trafficking, and the man with her had started out meeting her as a client. But after he met her and paid for her services, even after he had escorted her to a room, he couldn't go through with what he had intended.

Why? he wondered. He had, after all, gone there for that purpose and had paid for it.

Why? the girl wondered, confused but relieved.

He couldn't explain. Instead he asked the girl if she had registration papers, the legal requirement for all registered sex workers.

Breaking into tears, she told him her story in the best Greek she could manage. She had been trapped. She wasn't registered. She was a victim.

The truth broke his heart. He sneaked the girl out of the brothel and brought her to the police, who then transported her to our home.

The officer helping with the transition said that, in twenty years of police work, he had never seen such a thing. It was Christmas and we had our first client, the first woman rescued from trafficking through the work of A21.

Once again, Difficulty had sneered that there was no way, but God had made a way. And God just kept doing it. One morning, I woke up feeling burdened for girls from the seven "stan" nations—Afghanistan, Kazakhstan, Kyrgyzstan, Pakistan, Tajikistan, Turkmenistan, and Uzbekistan.

I wanted everyone I knew praying, so I posted on social media what God had placed on my heart. It was astounding to realize that in multiple time zones and every quarter of the globe, tens of thousands of women connected by social media channels began praying for girls trapped in the "stan" countries. They didn't know exactly what to pray for, but they knew who did.

Three days later, the police conducted a raid in northern Greece. Eleven girls were rescued from human trafficking, and some were brought to our home. They were from Uzbekistan.

When they poured out their stories to us, one said, "We prayed to the God of Europe." Her companions nodded in agreement. "'If you are real,'" the girl said they prayed, "'if you exist, God, come and save us. We have asked Allah to rescue us and he has not. So, Jesus, if you are real, send someone to help us.'"

That is the power of prayer. The power of the one true God.[24]

OUR GOD IS SO BIG

When we're convinced something is too hard, when everyone tells us that it's impossible, God brings us the lost who have been hidden. He paves the way for all the right permits. He leads us to the girls who have been forgotten. He answers prayer—theirs and ours.

When the consultants we hired told us that A21 would fail in Eastern Europe, they gave us the benefit of their experience and wisdom in a way that made perfect sense to them. They believed they were telling us the truth. They made a sound case for why we could not do what we felt God was calling us to do. But when we decided to obey God, we didn't enlist him on *our* side; we joined *his* side, and God plus one is always a majority. He's bigger than the bully Difficulty and greater than any giant.

When difficulties get in the way of our daring to do what God has called us to do, we must ask ourselves, *Who am I going to believe? The rational or the supernatural? The factual or the true? The giants taunting us or the Lord God Almighty?*

God wants us to choose him. He wants us to put our faith in him.

The Bible tells us that the great fathers in the faith—men like Moses, and Abraham before him—and the nation of Israel all got to the destinations God had ordained for them by faith.[25] Their journeys made no sense: leaving everything they had, the safe and familiar, trading the known for the unknown. Their journeys weren't rational, explainable, definable, or predictable.

Neither was ours. When we started A21, we felt like Abraham when God called him to a new assignment. "By faith Abraham obeyed when he was called to go out to a place that he was to receive as an inheritance. And he went out, not knowing where he was going."[26]

Following the call of God on our lives—whatever it might be—requires exercising our faith, and faith requires moving forward into the unknown. It guarantees running into the unexpected. The unpredictable. The outrageous. But it brings the miraculous.

Faith is required when you're in doubt, when you're in want, when things are difficult and unclear. "Faith," the Bible tells us, "is confidence in what we hope for and assurance about what we do not see."[27] It's the substance that makes the abstract tangible. The evidence of things we cannot see.

If we don't feel we have enough faith, God tells us how to develop more. "So then faith comes by hearing, and hearing by the word of God."[28]

- *We can't touch faith, but it can move mountains.* "If you have faith as small as a mustard seed, you can say to this mountain, 'Move from here to there,' and it will move. Nothing will be impossible for you."[29]
- *We can't see faith, but it can save us.* "It is by grace you have been saved, through faith—and this is not from yourselves, it is the gift of God.[30]
- *We can't pick up faith, but it can defend us.* "Take up the shield of faith, with which you can extinguish all the flaming arrows of the evil one."[31]

- *We can't stand on faith physically, but it can uphold us.* "Have faith in the LORD your God and you will be upheld."[32]
- *We can't always explain faith perfectly, but it is the fuel to our prayers.* "Whatever you ask for in prayer, believe that you have received it, and it will be yours."[33]

Faith is real and powerful. It can conquer kingdoms, administer justice, and gain what was promised. It can shut the mouths of lions, quench the fury of flames, hold back the edge of the sword, raise the long dead, end torture, and release the imprisoned.[34] Faith can take us from where we are to right where God wants us to go.

And yet how misleading our perspective can be when it comes to the things God has called us to do. When all we can see is problems, he sees possibilities. When all we can see is difficulty, he sees destiny. When all we can see is a disheveled woman dumping out her purse in search of her phone in the hubbub of a busy airport, God sees a person with a calling and a purpose and something big to do in a place inhabited by all kinds of giants. And he doesn't flinch. He just gives her faith, the kind of faith he gives to all of us. The kind that can make a way where there is no way.

When the consultants told Nick and me that A21 would never work in Eastern Europe, that it needed much more than a wing and a prayer to fly, we took only part of their advice—the prayer part.

Now we have offices all over the world. A21 works to raise awareness of human trafficking, establish prevention programs in schools and orphanages, educate the public, represent victims as legal advocates, give them refuge in aftercare homes, and offer them restoration through our freedom centers.

God is so much bigger than any difficulty we will ever face on the way to fulfilling our calling. He sees above and beyond any obstacle. No prayer is too big for him to answer, no problem too big for him to solve. There is nothing—absolutely nothing—our God cannot do.

I will never forget the day my daughter Catherine came home

from children's church singing the song "My God Is So Big." She ran around the house, singing it over and over. "My God is so big, so strong and so mighty / There's nothing my God cannot do [clap, clap]."[35]

Eventually the endless repetition began to get on my nerves. And just when I was about to say, "Catie, Mommy needs some quiet time—alone," I caught myself. Because of God's grace, the thought occurred to me, *What if this is all Catherine ever knows and believes about God? What if the truth in these simple lyrics is woven into the very fabric of her heart and every fiber of her being? Imagine what she could do if she truly believed that no difficulty, obstacle, or hurdle could defeat God's plan for her life. Imagine the difficulties she could overcome without a second thought.*

I wanted that kind of faith. So I began to sing right along with her.

My God is so big, so mighty and so strong. There's nothing my God cannot do.

I still face giants, but I'm determined not to be stopped by them. I don't focus on how big the giants are; I focus on how big my God is. I put my faith in God. I believe God's call on my life to reach the missing. "Go into all the world," he said.[36] Find them. Rescue them. Restore them.

He didn't say how. He didn't say if. He just said go.

You go and do the same with what he has called you to do. Start where you are, with what you have, however you can, believing that nothing is impossible.

With God on our side, our giants don't stand a chance.

With God on our side, we can live undaunted.

THE HOPE
OF OUR CALLING

*I pray that the eyes of your heart may be enlightened in order
that you may know the hope to which he has called you,
the riches of his glorious inheritance in his holy people.*
—Ephesians 1:18

April lay awake, listening to the other girls sleeping. Desperate for the rhythm of their breathing to lull her to sleep, she stared at the ceiling in frustration as the sounds seemed only to agitate her. Rolling to her side, pushing against the unforgiving wood floor, she wadded the threadbare blanket into a makeshift pillow and stuffed it under her head. Despite the attempt, she found it impossible to relax, not even a little. Her body ached and her head hurt, but as she kept trying to give in to the quiet, for the first time in months, she began to hear her own thoughts in the distance.

I can't live like this anymore. I've got to get out of here. I have to find a way.

Since she was just a teen, she had wanted to be free, to go back home, where it had been safe and secure, but the voice of her trafficker threatening her and promising to murder her family if she didn't comply haunted her into submission. It was the loudest voice in her head—day in and day out—and yet every now and then, when a quiet moment caught her by surprise, when no one was forcing her to do the unspeakable, she would hear her own thoughts crying out through the noise.

God, do you see me? Do you know where I am? Please help me.

Having been raised in church, April knew God, and the idea that God was there, somewhere, was all the hope she had. On this particular night, it seemed to be enough.

Staring at the keys lying on the dresser, she couldn't help but begin to imagine what could be, what would be, if she ran. It was a daring thought. Having been locked inside the apartment—just like she had been in every room in every city where she'd been moved back and forth from place to place for years—she fixated on them. If she dared to try to escape, then she would have to grab them without making a sound, without even scratching the surface of the dresser. She would have to walk silently between the other girls sleeping on the floor without waking them and unlock the door fast enough to open it and get out before anyone could stop her. And the consequences if she failed? The knot that had formed in her stomach only twisted tighter.

Getting out would be impossible. She knew that. She had seen other girls try through the years, and it never ended well. But the longer she lay there, staring at the keys, imagining what could be, the more impossible it seemed not to try. A force inside her began to rise up.

If I don't make it . . . She shuddered and silently cried out, *God help me make it. Help me.*

Easing herself up, she ever so slowly crept to the dresser and reached for the keys. Wrapping her fingers around them carefully, tightly, she silently picked them up. Turning toward the door, stepping cautiously, she moved through the girls, one after the other.

God, please help me get home. I have to get home.

So many times in recent months, she had thought about her family and how much she missed them. It had been five years since she met Monica—a kind girl, it seemed—who offered what appeared to be friendship, only it led to a nightmare. Unbeknownst to April, the promise of a work opportunity and the adventure of travel was just bait. She was lured into a trap, into a world she had never even known existed, especially since she lived in a land supposed to be the freest country in the world. Eventually, as Monica drew her in closer, April was taken by a trafficker, beaten and repeatedly raped into submission. For the next five years, she was moved back and forth across the United States. She lived every day terrified her family would be murdered. Terrified she would never see them again.

Hope had died inside of April numerous times. There were days when she didn't think she could take it anymore, and she wanted to end the nightmare she was living, even if it meant not living at all. But something would pull her back to thinking about her family and getting home.

Still quaking with fear but driven by a surge of hope, she turned the key in the lock. The sound seemed as loud as the pounding of her heart, but there was no stopping now.

April ran out the door, and she kept going, and going, and going. Her heart was beating faster than it ever had before, but for the first time in five years, she knew God's eye was on her and not her trafficker's. She knew she would be free.

Ducking into an alleyway, racing alongside some buildings, she quickly pushed inside an entrance. Seeing a restroom inside the hallway, she ran into it and locked herself inside. Collecting her wits, catching her breath, she tried to think of what to do next. Not knowing whether to cry or just breathe, she turned on the faucet and threw cold water on her face. Staring in the mirror, she saw something in the image looking back. A strength. A resolve. A courage she'd never seen. Yes, all the brokenness was still there. The pain. The loss. The abuse. But there was a desperation mixed with hope that she'd never seen before. She felt in control of something—herself perhaps—for the first time in years.

Risking it all once more, she cracked open the door. No one was in the hallway, but the sound of a laundry room at the end of the hall echoed with the chugs of washers and dryers. It was an apartment building. Of course. Thinking of who might be in the laundry room, April began to formulate a plan.

I have to find a phone.

After years of being unable to trust anyone, utterly afraid to tell the truth, April found a woman waiting for her laundry to finish a cycle. She asked to borrow her phone. That's when April called the police, and they called the FBI, who already knew her name. They had been looking for her for years. April's family had never stopped believing they would find her. They had never stopped praying. They had never given up hope. And truthfully, deep down, even when all felt hopeless, neither had April.

Within two weeks of being free from five years of horror, April reconnected with her family, and the FBI connected her with A21. With the help of A21 and our aftercare team, April spent another five years being restored and rediscovering what it means to truly live free and hopeful for a future. Her season of restoration was a process, a journey that our team had the privilege of walking with her. "After I was rescued, there were times when I felt so alone, like I was the only victim of human trafficking. And I would get so down. But one of those times, an A21 worker gave me a basket of toiletries, detergent, and other basic things you need, and when I said, 'Thank you,' she said, 'You're welcome. It could have been me. I could have been where you are.' When she said that, it just freed me even more and gave me even more hope. It made me determined that I was not going to keep thinking and feeling like a victim. I was not going to just sit there and let my trafficker win. I'm a survivor of this. I'm going to bounce back. She was right, though. It can happen to anyone. It could have happened to her."

Today April is helping other survivors by serving with A21. She has joined our team and assists our aftercare workers.

"I didn't go through all I went through to just walk away from it," April said. "I went through that experience so that I could help the thousands upon thousands still in that situation. I know what it feels like to be where they are."

April wants survivors to experience the same freedom and happiness she has found—to be reunited with their family, to wear a brand-new pair of shoes, to smile for the first time in years, to accept a job offer, to feel safe.

ON MISSION FOR THE MISSING

While human trafficking has gone on for centuries, it's no longer hiding in the shadows of history. Modern-day slavery is real, and victims are living in every city, in every country. They include girls like April, girls who used to live next door.

I will never stop being grateful that April didn't give up hope and that she managed to escape, and I will never stop being grateful that Nick and I didn't give up hope either. Otherwise A21 never would have been there for April.

As we built A21 through the years, there were plenty of opportunities to cave, to quit, to give up hope, especially early on. Doors were closed, people didn't follow through, plans failed, never mind the consultants' report that would sometimes remind us of how impossible it was. But because God had revealed to us that launching an anti–human trafficking organization was part of our calling, we kept moving forward, sometimes with nothing but our faith. So many times when we hit a wall, we would regroup, devise a new plan, make another phone call, reach out to a different government agency, and we just kept showing up until a breakthrough happened. We just kept moving forward step by step, undaunted.

What began when one person saw posters of missing women and children on a wall grew into a mission God has called an entire team to fulfill. Not long ago, as I stepped off an airplane in London's Heathrow Airport and made my way to baggage claim, I came face-to-face with how far we've come in the last ten years. Walking up to the carousel to wait for my luggage, I froze at the sight of one of our large-scale images on a lighted display. It was towering over me, in plain view, for thousands of people to see every day. It was part of our Can You See Me? campaign to bring awareness to the public, to teach people how to identify victims of human trafficking and alert authorities. A21 has these images on buses, in airport terminals, in subways, and in other public venues around the world. Standing there, I couldn't help but cry. I felt like I was seeing my calling come to life once more. What began in a regional airport in Thessaloniki was now a global campaign fighting for the missing in the biggest airports in the world. It felt like we had turned the tables on the enemy. We had mobilized the world to go and find the missing alongside us. We were no longer in the fight alone. We were no longer facing the impossible alone.

GOD HAS SENT US

So what about you? What has God called you to do? What comes to mind when you consider the word *called*, with its multilayered meaning of strategic purpose, specific intent, and concrete direction? Your calling is your assignment, your vocation. It's a purpose outside of yourself. It's how you light up your part of this world. It doesn't matter if you don't think you have the courage, the strength, the wisdom, the money, the influence, the experience, the education, the organization, or the backing. If God shows you something he wants you to do, you can do it. He doesn't call the qualified. He qualifies the called.

I wanted to share April's story—and all the stories in this book—to inspire you, to show you that every great endeavor starts where you are. It can be difficult to launch, but if your actions affect even one life, then it is worth whatever you have to push through with undaunted faith.

Once God opened my eyes to the horrors in this world, to the reality of human trafficking, my restlessness grew. The horrors were not in another time or place but next door, along my streets, in my community, and wherever I traveled. So I started where I was, with what I had, which was nothing more than a directive I felt led to follow.

Since then, I have learned so much, and not just how governments function or how law enforcement tackles trafficking or why such heinous crimes are so hard to convict. My eyes have been opened to some deeply personal realizations. When I've looked into the eyes of a Maria, a Nadia, or a Sonia, I've become so aware that their story could so easily have been mine. I had once been unloved, forgotten, and broken, left at a hospital with an uncertain future. What if, as number 2508 of 1966, I'd been born in Moldova or Bulgaria or Romania and left in an orphanage instead of a hospital in Sydney, Australia? What if I'd never been adopted by loving, kind, generous parents? What if those who took me home from the hospital had been traffickers? Something that really happens all too often. What if my abuse had never stopped, if I had never escaped it?

God alerted me to a kind of suffering in this world that imprisons men, women, and children, people who have become victims of sex trafficking, domestic servitude, or forced labor, and he called me to do something about it. I had no idea where to begin. No substantial resources to launch an NGO. No knowledge of what human trafficking really is or how prevalent it is. But I didn't let that stop me.

Even though my life seemed far removed from the lives of those who are trapped, pleading, broken, I didn't let that stop me. I realize that when I lay down at night to sleep, we are worlds apart. I am happily married, with healthy and happy children, living in a loving and safe home, able to come and go and travel the world with purpose and amazing opportunities to teach and to learn. My family and I have food, clothing, shelter, and healthcare. My future is filled with dreams, plans, goals, vision. I am free. Yet in the work of A21 and in my travels, I meet so many who are languishing, forgotten, without justice, love, hope, or any promise that their lives—or their children's—may someday get better.

Our situations could not be more different. All the more reason why it's imperative that I reach out and do everything I possibly can.

Our callings can be as different as we are, but we are all called to do something. Maybe God wants you to

- mentor young people in after-school tutoring programs
- reach out to women in recovery programs who need to hear, "Yes, you can"
- build a network for young moms and help them launch home-based businesses
- lead a neighborhood Bible study, providing a safe place for people to grow
- go back to school or start a business or change careers

Jesus prayed, "As you sent me into the world, I have sent them."[1] God has sent me, and he has sent you. He has sent us out with different callings, but every single one of our callings is to include reaching people. Loving them. Encouraging them. Serving them. Advocating for the poor, marginalized, and disenfranchised. Possibly rescuing them, if that's what they need. He wants us to help restore humanity, to seek and to save the lost. Over every person who is lost, God has written a word: loved.

God said he did not send his Son into the world to condemn the world but to save the entire world through him. Then Jesus commissioned us to go into that same world and to shine his light in the darkness so that others may be found and set free. What he did for us, he wants us to do for others.[2]

For when we were yet unloved, he loved us.[3]

Before we could be chosen, he chose us.[4]

When we were broken and damaged, feeding on bitterness and blame, he made us whole and showed us how to feast on forgiveness.[5]

When we had no hope, he became our hope.[6]

When we were overly busy with the cares of this world, he interrupted us to show us what is eternal.[7]

When we were lost, he found us and showed us that his mercy and justice will prevail.[8]

When we were disappointed, he sustained us to show us how disappointments can bring us to appointments he ordained.[9]

When we were afraid, he gave us courage, stood with us, and showed us how to illuminate the darkness with his light.[10]

When things got difficult, he pulled us along and pushed and carried us so that we could pull, push, and carry others.[11]

When Jesus said to go into all the world, he didn't mean to wait until morning or until you get the right job or find the perfect spouse or have raised the kids right or have your house in order or find a spare weekend. When Jesus said to go into all the world, he meant now.[12] To be a lantern in the darkness. A light in our world. To walk like him. To fulfill all that he's called us to do.

Unflinching in the face of disappointment.

Unshakeable in the face of our past.

Unafraid of the dark.

Unwilling to hold back.

Unhindered by our limitations.

Unashamed of our calling.

Unstoppable in the face of difficulty.

Undaunted in our faith.

Note: April's name has been changed in this account, and her story is a compilation of stories based on accounts from multiple victims of human trafficking, all in an effort to protect each survivor's identity and future safety.

ACKNOWLEDGMENTS

I will forever be grateful to all the people who helped make *Undaunted* a reality. This book would not be in your hands today without the help of my collaborative writer, Elizabeth Prestwood. I am a great believer that it takes teamwork to make any dream work, and that is definitely the case with my writing projects. I need help to get the thoughts that are in my heart down on paper in a way that connects deeply with you, my readers. Elizabeth is a gift from God to me and you in this process.

To my husband, Nick, and to our girls, Catherine and Sophia: I love that we are in ministry together as a family. We are Team Caine. I love that you are the ones I lean into and listen to. Your love, support, and sacrifice during the writing process of every book means the world to me.

To our A21, Propel, Zoe Church, and Equip and Empower teams, volunteers, partners, and supporters: Changing the world with you one life at a time is the greatest privilege and honor of my life. You are the ones who make every endeavor possible.

To Kristen Morse and Rebekah Layton: Thank you for reading each chapter, adding your insight and confirming facts and stories. Your contribution, like so many times in the past, was invaluable.

To "April": Thank you for being the inspiration for the epilogue and bravely sharing your story. Your courage and determination to overcome, to be restored, and to inspire other survivors keeps me going.

To the Zondervan team: After several books, you have most definitely become family. Thank you to Sandy Vander Zicht for getting this project off the ground, and congratulations on your retirement. You will be missed. To Stephanie Smith, for picking up the baton and taking this revised work across the finish line. I look forward to our future. Thank you, David Morris, for your leadership and belief in this project. Thank you, Tom Dean, Alicia Kasen, and Robin Barnett, along with the entire marketing team, for your dedication and commitment to launching yet another book.

To Max Lucado: For agreeing to write the foreword for the first edition and allowing us to reprint it in this revised edition. To this day, I am so deeply moved when I read it. Your words have been used so often by God to inspire and encourage me. It is one of the greatest honors of my life that you would so kindly add your strength to my message.

To my Lord and Savior, Jesus Christ: Thank you for healing me and showing me your plans, purposes, and call for my life. Thank you for giving me faith and leading me to live my life undaunted!

NOTES

Chapter 1: He Has Called Us

1. *www.vox.com/2015/6/29/8862583/greek-financial-crisis-explained.*
2. *www.thebalance.com/stock-market-crash-of-2008–3305535.*
3. Luke 4:18.
4. Rom. 1:1; *https://renner.org/devotionals/the-comforter-part-2/.*
5. *https://catalystleader.com/read/calling-or-career*; Gen. 2:15; 2:20.
6. Ex. 4:10, 13.

Chapter 2: I'm Not Who I Thought I Was

1. Ps. 139:13–16.
2. Isa. 46:10; Jer. 29:11.
3. Rom. 8:38–39.
4. John 3:16; 14:1–6.
5. Eph. 2:10.
6. Deut. 31:6; Ps. 46:1; 63:8; Heb. 13:5–6.
7. John 8:30–32.
8. 1 John 4:13–18.
9. Eph. 1:4–5.
10. Deut. 7:9; Ps. 86:15; 1 John 3:1.
11. Isa. 49:16; Luke 10:20; Ps. 139:16.
12. Isa. 46:4.
13. Heb. 6:19.

Chapter 3: Number 2508 of 1966

1. Gen. 1:27; Eph. 2:10.
2. Eph. 2:10.
3. 1 Tim. 6:12.
4. Deut. 31:6; John 10:27; Heb. 13:5.
5. NKJV.
6. Isa. 49:1 NKJV.
7. Ibid.
8. Mark 13:31.
9. John 3:5–8.
10. Eph. 2:10.
11. Ibid.
12. Isa. 43:1 NKJV.
13. Isa. 49:15–16.
14. 1 Peter 2:9.
15. 2 Cor. 5:17 NKJV.
16. Deut. 31:6.
17. Rom. 8:15.
18. Eph. 4:11–24.
19. Job 36:26.
20. Isa. 55:8–9.
21. Ps. 139:7–16.
22. John 15:16; Eph. 1:4.
23. Isa. 43:1 NKJV.

Chapter 4: He Healed My Hidden Wounds

1. Col. 3:13.
2. 2 Kings 5:1–19.
3. Acts 3:1–10.
4. Acts 3:11–26; Acts 4:4.
5. Matt. 18:21–22; Col. 3:13.
6. Phil. 4:8.
7. Phil. 3:12.
8. Phil. 3:13–14.
9. 2 Sam. 7:22.
10. Isa. 49:13.
11. Ps. 35:1.
12. Prov. 3:5–6; Ps. 20:7.
13. Gen. 50:20.
14. 2 Cor. 12:9.

Chapter 5: He Walked Me through My Disappointment

1. Ps. 145:17 NASB.
2. Ps. 139:7.
3. Jer. 33:3 ESV.
4. Deut. 31:6.
5. Luke 24:13–35.
6. Luke 24:30.
7. Matt. 28:16–20.
8. "Blessed Be Your Name," by Matt and Beth Redman. Copyright © 2002 Thankyou Music (PRS) (adm. worldwide at EMICMG Publishing.com, excluding Europe which is adm. by Kingswaysongs). All rights reserved. Used by permission.
9. Isa. 61:3.
10. Hab. 3:17–18.
11. 2 Cor. 10:5.
12. Heb. 10:23.
13. Ps. 145:18–19.

Chapter 6: I Overcame My Biggest Fear

1. Phil. 4:6–7 NKJV.
2. Deut. 31:6.
3. Phil. 4:8–9 KJV.
4. Isa. 46:10.
5. Matt. 14:22–33; Mark 6:45–56; John 6:16–24.
6. Matt. 14:29.
7. Matt. 14:30.
8. Matt. 14:31.
9. Matt. 28:19–20.
10. Matt. 28:20.
11. John 10:10.
12. Ibid.
13. Luke 1:26–38 KJV; Matt. 1:19–25 KJV; Luke 2:8–20 KJV.
14. 2 Tim. 1:7 NKJV.
15. 1 Cor. 2:16.
16. John 21:17.
17. Rom. 12:2.
18. Phil. 4:6–7 NKJV.
19. Ps. 27:1.
20. Isa. 41:10 NKJV.

Chapter 7: I Remembered What It Was to Be Lost

1. Luke 19:10.
2. Luke 15:4–7.
3. Luke 15:8–10.
4. Luke 15:11–32.
5. Luke 23:33–43.
6. Luke 19:10.
7. Luke 19:10.

Chapter 8: He Didn't Give Me a Caged Life

1. John 10:10.
2. 2 Cor. 6:11–13 MSG.
3. Heb. 11:1.
4. 2 Cor. 5:7.
5. Heb. 11:1 MSG.
6. Josh. 24:14–15; Deut. 30:19.
7. Heb. 10:23; 1 John 4:4.
8. Ex. 8:1–2.
9. Ex. 8:3–4.
10. Ex. 8:5–6.
11. Ex. 8:7.
12. Ex. 8:8.
13. Ex. 8:9.
14. Ex. 8:10.
15. Ex. 8:10–13.
16. Eph. 2:10 NKJV.

Chapter 9: I Awakened to More

1. *www.ushmm.org/wlc/en/article.php?ModuleId=10007056; http:// en.auschwitz.org/lekcja/1/; www.ushmm.org/wlc/en/article.php ?ModuleId=10005261; www.ushmm.org/wlc/en/article.php?Module Id=10005479; http://auschwitz.org/en/history/categories-of-prisoners*
2. *http://auschwitz.org/en/museum/auschwitz-prisoners/prisoner-numbers.*
3. Erwin Lutzer, *When a Nation Forgets God: Seven Lessons We Must Learn from Nazi Germany* (Chicago: Moody, 2009).
4. Luke 4:18.
5. Matt. 25:40.
6. Eph. 5:14–16.
7. Matt. 5:14–16.

8. Isa. 60:1–2 NKJV.
9. MSG.
10. Mic. 6:8 NKVJ.
11. Est. 4:14.

Chapter 10: Her Name Was Sophia

1. *https://uk.reuters.com/article/uk-portugal-girl/kidnapping-concern-for
   -missing-girl-in-portugal-idUKL0439120620070504.*
2. Luke 10:30 NKJV.
3. Luke 10:31–34 NKJV.
4. Gen. 50:20.
5. 2 Cor. 3:5–6 AMP.
6. Ex. 4:11–12 NLT.
7. Judg. 6:12.
8. Judg. 6:15–16.
9. Jer. 1:5.
10. Heb. 13:5.
11. Phil. 2:13.
12. Matt. 10:8.

Chapter 11: Nothing Is Impossible

1. 1 Sam. 17:16.
2. 1 Sam. 17:8–10.
3. 1 Sam. 17:11.
4. 1 Sam. 17:24.
5. 2 Tim. 1:7 NKJV.
6. 1 Sam. 17:26.
7. 1 Sam. 17:25.
8. 1 Sam. 17:32.
9. 1 Sam. 17:45–47.
10. 1 John 4:4.
11. Luke 18:27.
12. Rom. 8:31 KJV.
13. Matt. 28:20.
14. Deut. 31:6; Heb. 13:5.
15. Isa. 43:16–21.
16. Heb. 11:6.
17. Matt. 28:19–20.
18. 1 Sam. 17:47.

19. John 16:33 NKJV.
20. Luke 18:27.
21. 1 Sam. 17:45.
22. Eph. 6:10–20.
23. James 5:16 AMPC.
24. John 17:3.
25. Hebrews 11.
26. Heb. 11:8 ESV.
27. Heb. 11:1.
28. Rom. 10:17 NKJV.
29. Matt. 17:20.
30. Eph. 2:8.
31. Eph. 6:16.
32. 2 Chron. 20:20.
33. Mark 11:24.
34. Heb. 11:3–38.
35. Ruth Calkin, Nuggets of Truth Publishing © 1959, 2002.
36. Mark 16:15.

Epilogue

1. John 17:18.
2. John 3:17; 17:18; Matt. 5:16.
3. 1 John 4:19.
4. Eph. 1:4.
5. Col. 2:13.
6. 1 Peter 1:3.
7. 1 Peter 5:7–9
8. Luke 15
9. John 6:24–35.
10. John 1:1–5; John 8:12.
11. Matt. 28:18–20; Isa. 53:4–5.
12. Matt. 28:19.

Unexpected

Leave Fear Behind, Move Forward in Faith, Embrace the Adventure

Christine Caine

Is it possible to have peace in an uncertain world? To not only expect the unexpected but embrace it?

Most of us want to have life under control. But God wants us to anticipate the unexpected with a faith deeply rooted in his goodness. He wants us to know that because he is in control, we don't have to be.

In *Unexpected*, beloved author Christine Caine helps us walk into the life God has for us—unknowns and all. Using dramatic examples from her own journey, Christine offers real-life strategies and biblical inspiration to help us move from fear and worry about ourselves to hope and trust in God. As we learn new ways to manage disappointment, strengthen our hearts, and build our faith, we can enjoy a new adventure with God that is more fulfilling than any day we spend trying to anticipate what will happen next.

Stepping into our God-given destiny means stepping into the unknown, but we can embrace that calling because God knows it already. Nothing in our lives takes God by surprise. So even in the midst of personal upheaval, relational challenges, financial stresses, family transitions, career disappointments, and chaotic world affairs, we can expect God to be good and do good. What other expectation do we need to have? Listen to God's dare to trust him in every unknown of your life today.

Available in stores and online!

Unashamed

Drop the Baggage, Pick up Your Freedom, Fulfill Your Destiny

Christine Caine

Shame can take on many forms. It hides in the shadows of the most successful, confident, and high-achieving woman who struggles with balancing her work and children, as well as in the heart of the broken, abused, and down-trodden woman who has been told that she will never amount to anything. Shame hides in plain sight and can hold us back in ways we do not realize. But Christine Caine wants readers to know something: we can all be free.

"I know. I've been there," writes Christine. "I was schooled in shame. It has been my constant companion from my very earliest memories. I see shame everywhere I look in the world, including in the church. It creeps from heart to heart, growing in shadowy places, feeding on itself so that those struggling with it are too shamed to seek help from shame itself."

In *Unashamed*, Christine reveals the often-hidden consequences of shame—in her own life and the lives of so many Christian women—and invites you to join her in moving from a shame-filled to a shame-free life.

In her passionate and candid style, Christine leads you into God's Word where you will see for yourself how to believe that God is bigger than your mistakes, your inadequacies, your past, and your limitations. He is more powerful than anything you've done and stronger than anything ever done to you. You can deal with your yesterday today, so that you can move on to what God has in store for you tomorrow—a powerful purpose and destiny he wants you to fulfill.

Join the journey. Lay ahold of the power of Jesus Christ today and step into the future—his future for you—a beautiful, full, life-giving future, where you can even become a shame-lifter to others. Live unashamed!